# This We Can Believe

# THIS
# WE CAN
# BELIEVE

*Randolph Crump Miller*

HAWTHORN BOOKS, INC.
PUBLISHERS / *New York*

Dedicated to my students
through the years
and especially to

*Larry Axel*
*Gwen Langdoc Buehrens*
*Boardman W. Kathan*
*William Bean Kennedy*
*Sara Little*
*Neely McCarter*
*Charles F. Melchert*
*David S. Steward*
*Richard M. Trelease, Jr.*

# Contents

*Contents*

# *Preface*

We are concerned in these pages with what a person can believe as a Christian in the light of doubt and uncertainty, of scientific and political changes, and of recent developments in Christian thought. Many of us find that we question the values of our way of living, our democratic government, our technological breakthroughs, our friends, our God, and even ourselves. If we cannot have faith in something or someone outside of ourselves, we become cynical and pessimistic. The result is an underlying anxiety that paralyzes us in the seeking of meaning for our lives.

If a person is oriented to the world as pictured by modern science, if one is trying to build a life that has meaning in capitalistic, democratic Western culture, if the individual is seeking to be a Christian and yet remain a citizen of the twentieth century, there are problems to be worked out. To look at possible solutions to these problems is one of the purposes of this book.

There is a tremendous gap between the thinking of leaders among theologians, clergy, and laity and the ideas of most people who make up the bulk of church membership. This is the fault of the leadership, for with the best intentions they have watered down the discoveries of experts in the field of religious thinking, and as a result there is little orientation to sound beliefs for today. This book is an attempt to close this gap.

Another reason for writing this book is that religious education is at a low ebb. When the normal parent or church school teacher is faced with questions by children, the religious ignorance of this generation becomes obvious. Not only do we lack the resources to help younger people develop intelligent beliefs but there is also bankruptcy in facing moral questions. It is hard to lead children and young people to possible answers to their questions if we have no sound answers ourselves.

Another purpose is the main reason for writing any book: I have a point of view to present. I believe that we can state the essential beliefs of Christianity in terms that make sense today. The general point of view is that of *process thinking*, whereby we look on reality as a constant process of becoming and perishing, and in which God is at work as the basic structure of that process and as interacting with it. The method used is that of *empiricism*, which means that knowledge is based upon the critical and appreciative interpretation of our common human experiences. We need to be empirical, pragmatic, and pluralistic in our thinking about the realities to which religious beliefs point. I have described some aspects of this approach and of the people representing it in *The American Spirit in Theology* (1974). Such names as William James, Henry Nelson Wieman, Alfred North Whitehead, Daniel Day Williams, John B. Cobb, Jr. and Bernard Eugene Meland are significant for understanding this kind of thinking.

I have tried to write in language which is free from too much technical jargon and from sexist categories. However, Chapter 2 may be difficult for some readers and can be skipped or read after the rest of the book. Although I have not dealt specifically with the concerns of blacks, Chicanos, feminists, and the oppressed, I am aware that theology is culturally conditioned, and I have tried to avoid language which is not applicable to those with special concerns. There is a sense in which religion has special language categories or language games, and to speak of God and religion one must use these categories. I faced these problems in *The Language Gap and God* (1970).

Since 1936, I have been teaching in theological schools, often working part time as a pastor or educator or editor. With a dual concern for theology and religious education, I have been aware that one can speak of religious beliefs only in a context in which religious questions are being asked. Inert ideas that are not addressed to genuine questions have no religious effects. But dynamic ideas that are pointing to or showing what the reality of God is always have relevance. This book obviously can open up only a few areas of belief, and it may awaken the interest of the readers for further exploration; therefore, a list of nontechnical and technical books on various topics is appended.

My wife, as usual, has helped me gain greater clarity. Martha Bateman has read the manuscript to look for sexist terms, and her criticisms have sensitized me to the offensive nature of many theological terms. The Reverend Maurice Barry has read it and checked several details. I have acknowledged the publishers of the various books from which I have quoted the first time the book appears in the footnotes.

I have used translations of the Bible as follows:

CP  *The Cotton Patch Version of Luke and Acts.* Clarence Jordan. Copyright 1969 by Clarence Jordan. New York: Association Press.

G  *The Complete Bible: An American Translation.* Edgar J. Goodspeed and J. M. Powis Smith. Copyright 1939 by the University of Chicago Press.

NEB  *The New English Bible.* Copyright 1961, 1970 by the Delegates of the Oxford University Press and the Syndics of the Cambridge University Press.

PB  *The Book of Common Prayer.* 1928.

RSV  *Revised Standard Version of the Bible.* Copyright 1946, 1952, 1971 by the Division of Christian Education, National Council of Churches.

# This We Can Believe

# 1
# Your Faith and Mine

It is difficult to know what we can believe in these days. Many events in different fields have placed obstacles in the way of our older beliefs. We go to school or college and discover that secular education has little time for religion. We turn to modern science for an understanding of the nature of things and find that it is at least neutral toward religion. We discover that the religious beliefs we have inherited do not fit in with the newest discoveries of human knowledge, and often we are unaware of what modern religious thinkers are saying.

When we look at the world around us, our doubts about the goodness and love of God are increased. In a world of wars, of stress and calamity, where strife and suffering are evident and the rule of peace and justice the exception, there seems to be little room for Christian beliefs. After all, we ask, is not Christianity irrelevant to humanity's plight? We look at the church and discover that its record is not very encouraging. When the churches do seem to be doing something about poverty, or race relations, or liberation of women, or the condition of the oppressed, there is the threat of internal dissension. Most churches have failed to stimulate social legislation of any significance. The churches are concerned with petty things and internal problems and rarely have a sense of outreach or a concern for human failings beyond the purely personal. When they do turn to civil affairs, they develop an innocuous civil religion that asks God's blessing on things as they are, especially for the privileged groups.

Education, the world, and the churches contribute their shares to the conspiracy, probably an unconscious one, against ascertaining possible religious beliefs. The problem becomes acute when we reject all kinds of magic, miracle, and supernatural voices and yet put our trust in advertising slogans, jingoism, and sometimes astrology. In the past, the church could fall back on its claims of infallible authority of scripture or doctrine, or even on the appeal to miracle and magic. These methods may have validated the beliefs of our grandparents but they cannot validate the beliefs of our children.

We are asking for beliefs which are relevant to the current situation. We seem to be caught in the blind ebb and flow of history, and we want to know what meaning for us is to be found in these events. We are enmeshed in a web of local activities which endanger our families, our livelihoods, and our feelings of security, and we want to know why this happens to us. We face tragedy and despair and failure among those we love, and we need the hope and strength which the Christian religion promises. We see the temptations of power, arrogance, pride, and dishonesty among those in high and low places and wonder whether we need to follow such paths in order to survive. We begin to doubt the moral sanctions of society and the higher moral ideals of the church.

The purpose underlying the questions of belief and of the language of religion is the deeper one of finding an answer to our personal and social problems in terms of truth. We want to know what we can believe about the Bible, God, Jesus Christ, the church, human nature, prayer, the kingdom of God, and our commitment to the Christian faith precisely because the reality that underlies these beliefs contains the living waters of life itself. When these beliefs are stated in terms consistent with a modern view of the world, as pictured by some scientists, and with the social and political forces at work in the world today, they open to us the power and work of God in the world. We will see how Christianity can be understood in terms of our common human experiences, and we will interpret our religion by using our rational powers as well as our hopes and insights.

## CHRISTIANITY AND DEMOCRACY

The Christianity we know has arisen within a democratic society, and this was no accident. Democracy can exist without Christianity, as in ancient Greece and pagan Rome, but it was a democracy that depended upon slavery at the lower stratum of society. Furthermore, there has been Christianity without democracy throughout most of the history of Christianity. The Roman Church controlled an empire which, at best, was an enlightened monarchy. The Lutheran Church thrived in a Prussian state. Missionaries of all denominations have worked successfully in nondemocratic fields.

No culture has existed without religion of some sort at its center. The religious nucleus of a nation is usually the key to our understanding of its meaning and purpose. When a civilization begins to die, it is revived primarily by the coming of a new religion or the reforming of the old one. We can see this when the ruler or emperor or president ceases to embody the religious values for which a nation stands, and then we need to wait and see if some new or reformed religious vision will catch hold of the rulers and the citizens. There was a vision behind the National Socialism that led to the Nazi regime and the destruction of the old Germany. There is a religious nucleus, although in secular terms, behind the formation of Communist states. Such visions, whether they are right or not, have captured the religious emotions of those who seek a new order of politics and society.

American democracy also has a religious nucleus. It is to be found in the Jewish-Christian tradition as mediated through the Protestant movement, and centers primarily in a high view of human beings. This confidence is what makes possible a society based on the consent of the governed. The idea that people are free and equal can never be supported by political, economic, or psychological evidence, for it is perfectly obvious that all people are not equal in ability, opportunity, or freedom. The doctrine of human nature at the heart of American democracy is a religious concept, with recognition that all of us are under a God who is impartial. From the beginning, however, there was a realization that power can corrupt and that only a system of checks and balances can keep both leaders and followers on the right track.

The individualism that has developed in the United States partly because of this high doctrine of human nature has often led to distortions of the original purpose. So-called rugged individualism has tended to deny political and social responsibility, and even the churches have aligned themselves with an imperialism and a success-oriented capitalism that deny many people their rights. This has made possible power structures in the political and economic orders that submerge individual initiative in striving for justice. Thus, individual citizens are forced to combine into their own power groups in order to lobby for desired results.

The Jewish-Christian doctrine of human nature which undergirds the American theory of citizenship depends on two fundamental beliefs: the reality of a creative and loving God, and the worth of the individual person in the sight of God. Today these two beliefs are being challenged by an opposing culture which denies both the nucleus and the practices of democracy. Is the religious nucleus of American democracy strong, vital, and courageous enough to provide the morale and unity which this civilization needs in order to survive? If, as some historians think, Christianity has always spoken most directly in times of crisis, there may be hope that the United States will stand up under the stress and strain of opposition and injustice, of secular assumptions that attack religious foundations, of internal dissension, and, as the tensions are lessened, will express its fundamental beliefs in the rights of all as children of God. If this religious nucleus is submerged and loses its force, the United States will be in danger of succumbing to fascism or some kind of corporate state where these fundamental rights are lost.

Although democracy is the most satisfactory environment, Christianity does not depend on democracy for its existence. The alliance between the two is a relatively late historical development. Christianity is indigenous in almost every country in the world regardless of political structures. Christianity can survive, as it has in Communist states, even when it is forced to go underground. But the American form of democracy depends upon an enlightened form of the Jewish and Christian doctrine of human nature (and its implied doctrine of God) in order to maintain its vitality.

The Protestant tradition which was mixed with the American spirit is in sharp decline, and properly so, for it has not remained relevant to the rapidly changing society or the ways of thinking of most people today. The recognition that this is a pluralistic society and not a melting pot has changed our attitudes toward other religious claims. There are ethnic and racial and feminist claims that need to be recognized. A youth movement working toward the discovery of truth in various religious experiments needs to be taken into account. No longer can we think of ourselves as a chosen people with imperialist purposes that will be good for other countries. We need to rethink our religion, experiment with new forms of community, and provide new ways of finding meaning for our own lives and for the nation.

Some of the good things in our civil religion remain. The Declaration of Independence, the Bill of Rights, and the Fourteenth Amendment to the Constitution need to be kept as ideals which have never been more than partially implemented, for they stand as a protection against the encroachments on religious, social, and political liberty; and they point to that religious nucleus which can be shared by those of many faiths because the beliefs are generalized.

The problem of what we believe not only strikes to the heart of our individual problems but is also fundamental to our understanding of ourselves as a nation with a form of government that promises life, liberty, and the pursuit of happiness. We need to rethink and revitalize our Christian thought and life in order to give our culture a dynamic center which can withstand the forces that are threatening our survival as a republic.

## A PERSONAL APPROACH TO THEOLOGY

Religious belief is highly personal. It is derived from a number of sources, but it is filtered through many experiences of the individual. Coercion, authority, conditioning, and indoctrination may be part of the process, but it is we who respond to these forces and make our own decisions. To some degree a personal element enters into all knowledge, but it is crucial in the understanding of theology or philosophy.

Philosophers and theologians often recognize that personal factors corrupt their opponent's views, but they assume that their own conclusions are suitably objective. Occasionally, however, a philosopher is honest and perceptive enough to take account of the bias, limitations, and personal factors that are part of the process of thinking. William James wrote that "a philosophy is the expression of a [person's] intimate character, and all definitions of the universe are but deliberately adopted reactions of human character upon it."[1]

However, this does not eliminate the responsibility of the philosopher or theologian to be as rigorous as possible in the perception of data, the seeking of evidence from many sources, the careful use of logic and reason in the formulation of hypotheses to be tested, and the checking of all conclusions against further evidence. The personal element enters the process, and it needs to be checked by some kind of consensus with others who are competent in the field.

If we are going to be stimulated to think about our own religious beliefs as a result of reading about another's views, we need to know what kind of a person we are dealing with. When a theologian's personality or character is hidden behind a screen of seemingly objective statements, we often find ourselves puzzled, for we have no clues by which to judge the claims that are made. What kind of experience has this theologian had? What is the over-

1. William James, *A Pluralistic Universe* (New York: Longmans, Green & Co., 1909), p. 20.

all point of view from which the theologian examines the evidence? Is there reliance on supernatural revelation derived from the past and accepted on the basis of authority? Is the scientific view of the world taken seriously? Is the Bible, tradition, or an independent examination of the data from these sources and today's experience primary? Many approaches are possible, and they determine to a great extent the final results.

The overall point of view is important for a number of reasons. In the area of science, work is done according to assumptions about concepts, methods, and world view, often centering on important exemplars (key examples). These assumptions are called *paradigms*. We tend to observe what we expect to see and to ignore other data. Our overall theory is not proved false, because we select the data. Only when we can no longer ignore data that intrude on our consciousness, or when a rival paradigm clearly offers a better explanation of the data, are we likely to choose a new paradigm.

Yet we find that experience is important as a basis for our paradigm. We discover, for example, that members of different denominations, and even of different religions, can appeal to a generalized interpretation of particular religious experiences. We find that religious trust and commitment operate within a variety of traditions. As it becomes more difficult to accept the old paradigm and its interpretation of the evidence, we either reject it and move to another or we give up the attempt to understand and the paradigm loses its power and we are caught in a vacuum of unfaith.[2] Sometimes our paradigms are completely unreasoned and operate as fixations, and then we find that we cannot reason about what have been called *bliks;* they simply determine how we see and what we see.[3] For most of us, however, there are moments when we experience new disclosures and everything begins to fit together;

2. Ian G. Barbour, *Myths, Models, and Paradigms* (New York: Harper & Row, 1974), pp. 8–11, 119–146.
3. See Randolph C. Miller, *The Language Gap and God* (Philadelphia: Pilgrim, 1970), pp. 126–130.

9

this experience leads to a conversion to a new paradigm, for as the "light dawns" we are able to use the insight for a reevaluation of the data from a new perspective.[4]

What is offered here is a paradigm derived from a picture of the world consistent with modern science, but which is specifically religious in its orientation. It is my conviction that a paradigm for doing theology can be derived from a process view of reality, starting with human experience interpreted in terms of becoming and perishing, and extending to the whole universe. The starting point is the study of the relationship between human beings and a superhuman reality we call God. But even to assume that such a reality as God exists causes us to look carefully at our own experiences, to determine how we know that anything can be said to exist, to reflect on the meaning of these experiences, and then to build a world view that includes our religious beliefs as part of a coherent system of thought. Such an approach makes use of radical empiricism, pragmatism, and a pluralistic world view. Radical empiricism, as I understand it, is based on an analysis of the experience of both objects and relationships, of both fact and value, with a testing process to check any conclusions. The pragmatic aspects involve us in testing whether our ideas work, for a tree is known by its fruits and faith without works is dead. Unless we impose an arbitrary unity on our experiences from a rational point of view, it seems to me that there are always a lot of loose ends in this kind of thinking, and this leads me to be satisfied with a degree of pluralism within the dynamics of a process way of thinking. I see all experiences within the framework of the process of becoming and perishing, and God as an active entity within the process who also transcends the process as everlasting.

Religious beliefs lead to commitment or faith. A theology derived from experience is not an academic exercise divorced from the processes of daily living. If I believe that God is at work in some way in the cosmos, in history, in society, and in personal life, my

4. Ian Ramsey, *Christian Empiricism*, ed. Jerry Gill (Grand Rapids, Michigan: Eerdmans, 1974), pp. 159–176.

response should be to the reality for which the word *God* stands. I find that I have a vocation, a way of responding in my own style of living as a worshipper and active participant. I become a member of a community of worshippers who share a similar outlook, and seek with them to live out the meaning of my life. This involves me in decisions that are personal and social, ethical and political, and leads me to share this way of belief and action with others.

Readers of this book need some hints of how the writer came to such conclusions, in terms of a minimum of autobiographical information as well as theological method. We are formed to a great extent by early influences and significant disclosures in the face of decisions along life's way.

## INFLUENCES AND DECISIONS

My father's religious outlook was a major influence. He was an intelligent, liberal Episcopal clergyman. From the beginning I heard his portrayal of Jesus. Referring to Jesus and Levi, he said: "Our religion is not basically sad. I cannot blot out of my mind that feast made by Levi. Levi was a rich man. He made not a supper but a *feast* in his own house for Jesus. And Jesus was there *enjoying it all!*"

"I choose the *radiant Christ:* the one who saw beauty and goodness and truth in things and people, in whose heart was the eternal song and in whose character were virile sanctions worthy of all the lovely life that is to be!" This was not a Pollyanna optimism but an insight into the potential for goodness in human beings. He did not think that we bring out the best in people by damning them but by placing before them attractive goals. "Christianity is nothing more or less than the total impression made by Jesus on people. He seemed to have asked for nothing else. He expected to forward the cause of truth in no other way."

My father's parish provided an atmosphere in which we were free to seek new ideas and fresh ways of thinking. Against such a background, I was free to ask questions, and when I discovered that my father as a committed Christian was open to the reformulation and even the discarding of certain beliefs and was aware of scientific advances and the political implications of Christian living, it was easy for me to begin thinking on my own.

By the time I reached Pomona College, I had decided that I should enter the ministry. While in college, I learned that my mother had multiple sclerosis, and this led to a reconsideration of my belief in God as all-powerful and all-good. How could a good God permit this? In my course with Prof. Robert Denison, I was exposed to the thinking of William James, John Dewey, and Henry Nelson Wieman—among others. It was James who spoke directly to my problem. I began to see the universe pretty much as he did, as a pluralistic process of interrelationships, in which God is at work but not in complete control. If I could take seriously the fact that God has an environment, is limited in power, faces opposing forces, and works against evil that is also real, I could find a place for a God of love in the face of my mother's illness. This approach to the problems of suffering and evil, which we find today in the thinking of the process theologians, became a part of my new paradigm and remains as an important factor in my understanding of God's relation to the world.

James became one of the most important influences in my philosophical and theological thinking. I responded to his interpretation of radical empiricism which took seriously the existence of external relations and thus moved beyond the empiricism of Hume and others; I liked his pragmatism as a basis for testing the truth of one's beliefs; and I saw a connection between his interpretation of religion and my own, for sometime during those years I had experiences which I would later call (with F. S. C. Northrop) an awareness of "the undifferentiated aesthetic continuum." James' pluralism also attracted me. It seemed to me that he was always willing to take into account any data that came along, without forcing them into a fixed a priori system. It led him to believe in a loose-jointed universe and what he called a "piece meal" supernaturalism. There was, for me, an empirical basis for what James called the "divine More," and this could serve as a basis for my overbeliefs (based on speculation beyond the evidence).

These influences were strengthened during my graduate work at Yale. The most influential of my teachers was Douglas Clyde Macintosh, who spoke of "theology as an empirical science." I never agreed with the use of *science* as a description of theology, but I thought of the scientific spirit as an adequate synonym. Macintosh was interested in *how* we know as well as in *what* we know; he was much more systematic than James and also was critical of the positions of other philosophers and theologians. When it came time to write my dissertation, Macintosh led me into an investigation of the empirical theology of the Chicago school and especially of Henry Nelson Wieman. I found myself in partial agreement with Wieman, but I saw the need for a superstructure consistent with the empirical evidence yet beyond the realm of verification (which Macintosh called "reasonable belief" and "permissible surmise"). These studies served as the background for my writings since then, most notably in *What We Can Believe* (1941) and *The American Spirit in Theology* (1974).

During the time I taught at the Church Divinity School of the Pacific (1936–1952), I attempted to refine this kind of thinking, especially by working in the thought of Whitehead, Hartshorne, and other process thinkers. Much of what I thought was tested in the work of a parish. I had always been interested in Christian education and began to teach courses in this field. This led to a study of the relation of theology to education, and the result was *The Clue to Christian Education* (1950). I used more traditional language in that book, with more emphasis on the givenness of the Christian tradition, but I believe that it was consistent with my basic theological method.

By then, my faith had had another difficult test. My young wife, the mother of our four children, died from polio in 1948. What I discovered was that I did not need to blame God or to question God's love, for my earlier theological thinking had provided a basis for my acceptance of her death. This did not lessen the tragedy of undeserved and premature death or ease the grief, for nothing does that, but it enabled me to accept her death without bitterness. The deity I knew through experience (Macintosh's "right religious adjustment" or Northrop's "undifferentiated aesthetic continuum") was "a very present help in time of trouble." When I had to preach to my congregation two weeks later, my topic was "The Love of God."[5]

Two other experiences round out the picture. Both have to do with disclosures. I was in Virginia for some lectures, due to a chance invitation after others had refused. While there, also by chance, I met a young widow. Our meeting was so brief that normally no one would notice it. Yet both of us saw the significance of that occasion. There was some kind of disclosure to which we both responded. Call it chance, call it intuition, call it love. Within a year we were married.

Finally, there was the offer to come to Yale. We were happy in Berkeley in 1951. We had brought together our two families and they were adjusted to the local situation. The struggle was between theological and educational interests, and I was torn between them. I was assured that Yale wanted a theological approach to education, and after thinking it over I decided on Yale. It was not an immediate disclosure, as were the decisions to enter the ministry, to accept a position in California, or to follow up on my meeting with Lib. But God works through our struggles out of which decisions may come as well as through intuitions that need further testing.

Theology grows with one's experiences, even simple ones such as I have recounted. Every event could be accounted for on secular grounds if one had a secular paradigm through which one looks at the evidence; but for me this would be too simplistic. I want to be tough-minded, but I want to be open to what I think the data are telling me, and this fits into my empirically based, process-oriented, Christian paradigm. From one perspective, the events I

5. See Randolph C. Miller, *Living with Anxiety* (Philadelphia: Pilgrim Press, 1971), pp. 157–162.

have recounted were due to chance; from another they were the opportunity for emerging novelty in my life; and perhaps this is what we mean by guidance—taking advantage of novel episodes in one's life to further the values that are moving from the potential to the actual mode.

## COMMITMENT

For me, the word *commitment* is a key to the meaning of faith. It means that we are involved in a relationship of trust, of a pledge, of being bound to someone. When we give ourselves to God in trust, there is assurance that a covenant exists that promises preservation from ultimate evil. On the human side, we agree to seek and do what is highest and best, what we consider to be consistent with God's aims; this commitment is to God, not to any set of ideals or concepts, yet it is tied in with directions for action. The commitment is a form of loyalty, and the certainty lies in this relationship and not in the theological ideas or system that point to the reality of God.

Our commitment provides the certainty. Our beliefs cannot do it, because our testing of concepts depends on our interpretation of the data and our generalizations are based upon incomplete evidence. The most complete revelations of God are limited by the finite capacity of human appreciation, and even in Jesus Christ we find only as much revelation as human beings can reveal and absorb. But if our knowledge about God is always tentative, that does not leave us without certainty. The little that we do know about God is enough to require our absolute loyalty. We are able to revise our beliefs about God in the light of the evidence, but we do not revise God.

Faith involves three elements: right belief, commitment, and action. By right beliefs we mean those which point to and show us approximations of reality, beliefs that can be tested empirically within the paradigm or perspective that we have adopted. We may hold such beliefs and at the same time examine them and sometimes doubt them, so that we may refine them. Granting that we have attained some knowledge of God as the one who sustains us in our search for meaningful living, who is the transforming and creative process that enters our lives, what are the conditions for entering the right relationship with this sustaining power?

The word *faith* goes back to *tie* or *ligature.* Faith is the commitment of the total self to the process which makes possible creative living. Faith is a decision to follow the leading that comes from the relationship with God. God as a sustaining and integrating power in our search for meaning is a factor in our common human experience. Our faith does not create God or provide for our beliefs, for faith is a relationship of trust between actual entities. When we make a free and affirmative response by committing ourselves to that process we call God, we are making a choice in loyalties which may cost us some earthly values. It takes courage to make this commitment. There is risk, because such an adventure does not carry guaranteed results. There is no assurance of continuing victory but only that one is on the right side. There may be hope of final victory, but hope is not assurance.

The paradox of this approach is that although we must have enough knowledge of God to discern God's trustworthiness, it is only after the action of commitment that we gain greater knowledge of God. Faith creates its own data. Knowledge is the result of experimental activity, and as faith issues in action it opens up new vistas of the nature of God. Faith in one sense precedes the fuller knowledge of God, for the more we grow through the natural means of God's grace, the more our capacity for knowledge is increased.

Faith, then, issues in actions which verify (or do not verify when it is misdirected) the original hypothesis. Faith is a form of readiness to be a participant in the response to the emergent riches issuing from God's activity. There is a spontaneous goodness about a profoundly religious person (whether one professes to be religious in a conventional way or not) that is contagious. Others respond to it and take up similar attitudes.

Some theologies have seen human beings as passive in relation to God, so that freedom is actually denied. But if God's grace is persuasive and not irresistible, then the human response is an act of freedom. Instead of being conscripted by a heavenly monarch, we volunteer to enter God's service. Even more than like a mighty army, the fellowship of faith is like a family. When Jesus called his disciples, he used no compulsion, no threats, no guarantees. He said simply, "Follow me." Our faith means that we have accepted God's call. "If you know these things, blessed are you if you do them" (Jn. 13:17,RSV).

## THE BIBLE

The theologian who is a radical empiricist, a pragmatist, and has a pluralistic world view is also concerned that the Bible have a central place in theological construction. This recognition of the significance and authority of the Bible, however, takes on a hue that is different from that of the literalist or authoritarian. The Bible may be interpreted in terms of the acts of God, but only against the background of the findings of biblical scholarship, of seeing the passages of the Bible in terms of their situation at the time they were written, of reinterpreting passages seen from an early world view to be consistent with the world view of today, and interpreting this evidence in terms of both the human search for God and the record of God's action in history culminating in the story of Jesus Christ.

This point of view relieves us from the responsibility of defending or attacking the Bible in toto. The authority of the Bible rests simply on the discovery that it is so often right. In it we find the revelation of God's acts, nature, and will, because the history of Israel is replete with events which have been appreciated by illuminated minds capable of interpreting God to the people. God speaks to us through the Bible, because we find in it the spiritual nourishment which builds a life rich with meaning. As human situations approximate the historical backgrounds of the various biblical passages, their relevance becomes acutely obvious.

From the practical point of view, the Bible has a value far exceeding its literal significance. Because it provides a historical statement of religious development, because it gives us dynamic and vital interpretations of the human search for God, it provides for the modern person the point of departure for theology. Our theology is biblical, not in the sense of being limited to the Bible, but in the sense that no theology can be Christian without taking into account what the Bible says. It is the primary source of Christian theology. All the diversities of Christian belief claim the Bible as their source, and this places upon us added responsibility to deal intelligently with all that can be known about the Bible.

The Bible is not person-centered, for, although it is a record of the human search for God, the emphasis is on God. It provides historical data open to human interpretation, but it also recounts data that we interpret as acts of God. The message from God is received by the men and women of the Bible, sometimes muted, sometimes distorted, and sometimes with amazing clarity. A theology based on radical empiricism must use the data of the Bible with special recognition of their value.[6]

We are concerned with the way in which Christian theology can be understood in today's world, so that Christianity may be interpreted in terms of a world view derived from current knowledge, taking seriously the scientific and humanistic studies, the structure of a democratic society, and the new values emerging in the struggle for a greater degree of social justice. To me, this means working through the methods of empirical theology and process thinking to create a set of Christian beliefs that a modern person can find meaningful. This is not an attempt to make belief or faith easy, but to invite you to a difficult and exciting adventure. To the extent that this is an expression of the character of the writer as well as of the facts of living religiously today, readers can judge for themselves.

6. See Randolph C. Miller, *Biblical Theology and Christian Education* (New York: Charles Scribner's Sons, 1956).

## RELATIONSHIPS

My work in Christian education has led me to emphasize what has been called a "theology of relationships." Because of the significance of relationships between people as a means of reaching spiritual health, because of the evidence that the effectiveness of teachers is in terms of their contagious faith, because of the "I-thou" emphasis in the achieving of community, we begin to understand how God's grace works through human channels. The love, the forgiveness, and the redemptive and transforming power of God reaches persons chiefly through other persons.

Part of the evidence for this is found in the study of religion in the family. The earliest influences on a child are a reflection of parental faith in action, and this carries over into the period where words may either validate or contradict the claims of love. This becomes a way of interpreting social action on a broader scale; for the achievement of social justice, which historically has been considered as a representation of God's will in action, comes about as a result of intentional actions by individuals and groups. The breakdown of the social order can be interpreted as an expression of God's judgment. The Bible represents God as raising up nations to punish Israel for its wrongdoing, as well as calling upon Israel to achieve social justice.

Looking for evidence of God's work in and through people is consistent with an incarnational approach to the work of God. If we are to take Jesus seriously as a focal point of Christian faith, we need to have some understanding of how God works through people before we can use such language as "the Word became flesh and dwelt among us." Only then do we begin to perceive God's ingression in the person of Jesus Christ.

Human experience reveals a mixture of values through interpersonal experience, and thus we come to a view of human beings as an equally strange mixture of responses to the aims of God in the world. Persons are capable of magnificent deeds of love, justice, and sheer goodness, and we tend to ascribe such activities to the influence of God. But they are equally capable of expressing hatred, of betraying both friends and enemies, of perpetrating injustice, and of being malevolent, and we tend to ascribe (with equal logic) such behavior to the influence of demonic powers. It is easy to get caught in an oversimplified dualism and to ignore the complexities in the analysis of human behavior.

I am convinced that an examination of human behavior, of social relations, and of interpersonal experience will point to the transforming and creative presence of God. The empirical bent of mind in my own person requires this as the basic starting point of any system of religious beliefs. These data are complex and often contradictory, but they provide the foundation for developing concepts, theories, and speculations about the nature of the world and of God. We now turn to a consideration of the methods to be used.

# 2
# How to Test Our Beliefs

The function of our beliefs is to provide direction, perspective, and integration for our lives. They function in this manner whenever the object in which we believe receives our commitment and trust. If our beliefs are wrong, we are plunged into the abyss of error, tragedy, and destruction. If they are unsubstantiated, we cannot be sure that the direction in which they point is the correct one, and we are taking unnecessary risks. If they are right, we may be certain that we are on the side of the best that humanity, the world, and God can offer us. If our beliefs are fully tested and shown to be as certain as human knowledge can be at present, the object of our devotion has a claim to all that we are or can be.

Our beliefs need to be understood from two points of view: their sources, and their present status as knowledge. Without some comprehension of the sources, we have no way of setting up satisfactory tests, for religious beliefs are not tested in a day or by a single individual. Although the origin of a belief is no guarantee of its validity, it provides valuable hints. With this background, we are able to test it in the light of its history. It is impossible, for example, to reach adequate knowledge of the person and work of Jesus Christ without an understanding of the historical evidence, including his Jewish heritage.

## THE SOURCES OF OUR BELIEFS

There are four major sources of our beliefs as Christians. They come to us from tradition, from the Bible, from nonreligious knowledge, and from our common human experiences.

The first and primary source of belief is tradition. Christianity is an historical religion, and no one who partakes of the heritage of Western civilization can miss fully this influence. The average Christian today grows up in a particular cultus, and in gaining a sense of the ethos of one's own religious body one inherits beliefs, attitudes, and ideals which determine one's general religious outlook. Those outside Christianity do not remain free from its influence. To a certain extent this is a good thing, for it is patently impossible for all people to start over again in each generation without the benefit of this heritage.

But tradition is notoriously undependable, no matter how hallowed with age. This is true for at least five reasons: (1) Tradition is just as capable of passing on errors as of transmitting truth. It tends to crystallize symbols and myths into dogmatic statements, so that what was once a pictorial representation of reality becomes a literal statement of untruth. (2) Tradition does not afford the complete objectivity which has been claimed for it. Even in the most traditional groups, a selection must be made among the various traditions, and this involves the subjective choices of the selected authorities who determine what must be believed. (3) Our present knowledge of the limitations of the tradition-makers and the creed-makers does not set them up as the experts we have been led to believe they were. On the most significant questions they disagreed among themselves, and their statements were often deliberately one-sided in order to exclude certain heretical branches of the church. (4) The acceptance of traditional beliefs tends to discredit recent discoveries or restatements, in spite of the accuracy of later formulations. Traditional beliefs are guarded against the exacting criticism which must be demanded of all modern religious thinking. (5) Even when tradition is the channel of transmitting true beliefs, what is accepted is at best by intellectual assent. Tradition does not give the assurance necessary for a vital religious faith, for faith depends upon more than beliefs, demanding the individual's sense of the presence of God leading to commitment.

The champion of tradition has been the church, and throughout the ages it has been the church which has preserved Christian doctrine from destruction. We could wish that the church might have saved more of the early Christian writings than those found in the New Testament, but the church is to be thanked for what was saved. The church has been interested in conserving the past rather than in creating the future, so that it has not always served the real needs of humanity. We need to steer a central course between the bonds of tradition and the snares of our individual conceits, and the church today needs to be both more careful and more courageous in its handling of the past.

Tradition is an invaluable storehouse of expressions of religious beliefs and practices, but in itself it contains only suggestions of possible beliefs as guides to action. It contributes to modern beliefs and faith only as it is rephrased into the vocabulary of modern communication and is verified and validated in the present. To some people such changes in both language and concepts may seem revolutionary, whether in the field of liturgy or social action. At the same time, simply because it is tradition, we deserve to give it considerate treatment and to gain perspective on the present through the past. We must not be too impatient with these older concepts and practices just because they do not seem to fit the immediate situation.

A second source of belief and particular source of tradition which is binding to some extent on all Christians is the Bible. The record of the experiences and beliefs found there provides a basis in history for almost all traditional beliefs. But even in this sacred realm, the beliefs must be retested, restated, and dressed in modern concepts and translations. The reason the Bible is normative for Christian beliefs is not because it has supernatural authority, but because the experiences and testings of people through the ages have validated certain portions as God's revelation. Thus, it comes to have a unique authority as we understand more fully its origin and purpose, but even biblical beliefs cannot become a basis for faith without independent verification in present experience.

Within the Bible, the teachings of the New Testament have usually been treated with less critical acumen than those of the Old Testament, but even the Old Testament studies by Christian scholars have not often done justice to the Jewishness of Old Testament religion. The portrayal of Jesus as the Christ in traditional doctrines has not always done justice to the New Testament evidence. For example, it cannot be shown that all of Jesus' reported teachings are free from error, and if he was wrong, for example, in his specific statements concerning the end of the world, it is conceivable that he was wrong on other counts. We revere him and his teachings, and we find in him the center of our devotion, but we have no right to accept beliefs about him uncritically. Jesus' teachings have been ratified by experience many times, and even where many have doubted him subsequent events have shown him to be right after all, but it is difficult to avoid the conclusion that he may have been wrong occasionally. So we must apply the same critical discernment to the discovery and validating of his teachings and the teachings about him as we do to all biblical and church traditions.

Third, general secular knowledge provides data which may have religious significance. It was not an accident that Thomas Aquinas built his theology on the secular philosophy of Aristotle, or that process theologians today build on the philosophy of Alfred North Whitehead. We must know the world if we are to have any accurate knowledge of God. We do not identify God with the world, as in pantheism, but as we know the world we also come to know God. When we spell out our way of looking on the world, we are setting up the environment for our religious thinking. In other words, religion without metaphysics is impossible except as a theological abstraction. If we cannot find God in the order of the skies or the breaking of an atom, we are not likely to find God at prayer meeting or at mass. As our inherited beliefs were fitted into what is now an outmoded metaphysical framework, so it is obvious that our beliefs today must be consistent with our picture of the world.

The fourth source of our beliefs is our interpretation of common human experience, particularly as it is exemplified in personal experience. As in the fields of music or painting, the meaning and validity of religion lie in personal appreciation and verification.By their fruits you shall know them and by your fruits shall you know yourself. Religion must be grounded in the experience of persons. Of course, we must have objective tests by which to measure our experiences and norms by which to judge them. Our criteria emerge from joint efforts to evaluate experience.

We may take the authority of the expert in science, but in the field of religion even the authority of the expert cannot make belief live. The final experiment is that of life itself, and no one can do this by proxy. Each individual must make it for one's self or take the consequences. It can be postponed, but not indefinitely. Sometimes the beginning of the experience comes in the normal process of growth, but frequently it takes a crisis which demands a decision, and this opens the door to the experiment which must be made.

Beliefs held to be true in one century are reformulated, reinterpreted, enriched, or perhaps discarded in the next. In no field of human knowledge, not even religion, are there fixed truths. Static beliefs cannot apply for very long to a process which is constantly changing, cannot take account of new experiences or even of new perspectives on familiar data, and cannot point to future discoveries. Christianity's enemies are those who say that Christian beliefs never change, for they have been changing for almost two thousand years. The reality to which the word *God* points is believed always to be present in existence, although even God may change if God is process, but certainly our concepts which point to God need to be in constant revision. The certitude which makes faith possible lies in the relationship between God and us, while the ideas and concepts are constantly revised. Yet we need to test those beliefs which we do hold and which guide our actions, and this means that we need to see clearly what the criteria are.

## THE TESTS OF OUR BELIEFS

Our concepts should be approximations of the reality toward which they point. The beliefs that we have derived from tradition, the Bible, secular knowledge, and our interpretation of the data of experience need to be refined, double-checked, and reasserted in changed forms according to an adequate theological method. In all of these circumstances, there is a record of experience and interpretation, although this may not be immediately clear. In emphasizing the importance of relying on experience, a distinction is made between the data and the interpretation. Data are selected, based upon the purpose in mind, and then they are given some kind of rational and pragmatic coherence and consistency, so that what is asserted is tied in with the rest of our knowledge.

A number of tests have been suggested. Some people claim that we know "by faith," but it is never clear what this means except that they refuse to abide by the criteria normally used. Others say that we know by revelation, but this always throws us back to some other tests to determine whether a genuine revelation has occurred and been assimilated and interpreted properly. Many people rely on authority, but consent to authority may mean resigning one's own responsibility, unless the authority has been responsibly chosen. Authority is often only the consensus of a group of authority figures, who may or may not lack theological expertness. Some say that religious experience is enough, but this is mere subjective certitude unless other factors are brought in to determine both the data and the interpretation. A popular modern assumption is that if a belief works it is true, but many beliefs subsequently shown to be false have worked for a time to meet certain needs. There has been frequent reliance on intuition, but intuition is not a test of truth, although like religious experience it may provide significant data for interpretation.

While many tests have been suggested for establishing the truth of religious concepts and some of them have value, the one that has been of significance for me has been the method of observation, experimental behavior, and reason. This method is associated with the names of Douglas Clyde Macintosh, Henry Nelson Wieman, Bernard Eugene Meland, and Daniel Day Williams. It is a limited method and does not provide us with as much knowledge as we would like. When this process is used critically and appreciatively, and is repeated often enough in varying situations and even in different religious traditions, the resulting concepts will provide sufficient practical certainty for the guidance of life. It does not eliminate intellectual and religious risk, its results never eliminate an element of tentativeness, but it provides as much certainty as we find in any experiment of life.

This is the method known as empiricism. It consists of five steps: (1) It begins with the selection and gathering of the data of direct experience. (2) This is followed by experimental behavior and analysis of the data, thus discovering some patterns in the data that we need to interpret. (3) By the use of our constructive imagination we formulate hypotheses or concepts which explain or account for the data. These concepts become tools for handling other experiences and relating them to what is already established. (4) The concepts are tested to see if they are coherent in themselves, if they are consistent with the generally accepted body of knowledge, if they work, and if they actually explain the original experience. (5) On the basis of these findings, we can make rational inferences which carry us beyond the immediate experience and explain what is beyond experience.

Experience includes sense experience, but is to be understood on a broader scale. We not only experience things, but we also experience relations between events; thus our experience is radical. We often have a sense of the whole before we perceive particulars, and this vague feeling for the whole is a broader type of experience. Our experience is often appreciative, carrying with it an open awareness and a sense of "thickness" that takes us beyond the immediate moment. There is an appreciative consciousness which is primarily aesthetic, so that a rich fullness of experience frustrates our attempt to be exact.

There is a "vague affective tone" at the basis of experience. There is a feeling or concern or grasping which is an activity of the whole body and not just the senses. Whitehead calls this feeling a "prehension." It is a feeling by which one entity is related to another; it can become very complex. The use of the word *know* in the Bible to refer to both sexual intercourse and to knowledge of God indicates something of this feeling tone of a prehension. It is a kind of empathy for others. In its physical form it may be unconscious; in its mental form, as when we grasp the objective form of a potential that is not yet actual, it is conscious. The whole body experiences, and there is a feeling of closeness, as when we are told, "You will know that I am in my Father, and you in me, and I in you" (Jn. 14:20,RSV). In this usage, we can say that we prehend God and God prehends us.[1]

If we understand experience in this broader meaning, the empirical method can be applied to almost any kind of knowledge both in the sciences and the arts. In the sciences, the experiments can be controlled and manipulated, but sometimes the "thickness" of experience is not accounted for. In other fields of endeavor, the behaviors being observed are so constant that dependable results may be obtained. In studies of human behavior, we can predict a general outcome although we expect variations by individuals. In religious living, we deal with the aesthetic and feeling side of experience with greater depth, we are concerned with an intimate relationship between God and the variable human being, we are making value judgments and predictions in terms of the emergence of new values, and therefore the results are not nearly so constant as in the sciences, but this method does lead to religious knowledge.

The knowledge that comes in this way is limited, but it is the verified knowledge which is essential to any system of thought. It tells us how things or entities *behave,* whether we are talking of chemical ingredients, plants, human beings, or God. If we assume that an entity is what it does, which is a reasonable assumption, we have an approach to knowledge of God. Even in our knowledge of other persons, we are evaluating by the way the other behaves.

Although all religious knowledge comes in this way, it does not eliminate the view that God is the revealer. If the claim that God

1. See Alfred North Whitehead, *Process and Reality* (New York: Macmillan, 1929), pp. 337–338.

acts is the basis for judgment, as many biblical theologians claim, this becomes a source for the data about God. Even those who insist on the supernatural source of revelation agree that human minds have to interpret what has been revealed. Many would claim that God is the source of many insights in such secular fields as science or music or art, although the genius of the scientist or musician or artist is essential, so it is not unreasonable to suppose that religious geniuses have insights in their field which are no less a gift of God because they are the perceptions and insights of particular persons.

This does not eliminate specific revelations. In the life of Jesus, we can see now what no one had seen with such clarity before. There is nothing before or since the revelation of God in Jesus Christ which is its equal. When people speak of God today, Christ-likeness becomes one of the attributes. When people are confronted by Christ (however this might be interpreted metaphysically), they perceive that which they had not even imagined before. They begin to understand what is meant when it is said that "God was in Christ reconciling the world to himself." People find here in this kind of experience the transforming power of God, and so they say that they are saved through faith in Jesus Christ.

## Beyond Empiricism

This method of relying on experience and its interpretation is limited and can become dangerous. It is limited because it does not account for all the facts and does not always probe deeply enough into the claims of religious imagination. Those through whom revelation has come have rarely been self-conscious empiricists, and they have always thought in terms of overtones and imagery which empiricism cannot deal with. Very few people can live religiously or speak about such living without the aid of symbols, models, myths, poetry, and liturgical language which quickly move beyond the limits of empiricism. Revelation is a form of experience in which a particularly sensitive mind grasps the significance of events which might be overlooked by the less appreciative or perceptive. When the meaning and value of these experiences are signified to those who otherwise might not perceive them, these latter come to a fuller understanding of them. In this way, revealed concepts, given only to the few, are tested by the common experience of groups of people. Religious seers, however, are never conscious of the tests of their experience. They see the whole of their experiences and interpret them uncritically and almost unconsciously. Because of this, there are overtones in their experiences which are real to them but which cannot be conceptualized even in their own minds. Furthermore, they are unable to distinguish what they have projected onto the experience, culturally or psychologically. They resort to poetry, parable, myth, and imagery of various kinds in order to formulate the deeper meanings of their visions. Even then, because of their finiteness and the fullness of the source of their experience, something of vast importance seems to be lost to consciousness. Also, confused with these overtones of vast importance are the projections of the subconscious mind which are purely the product of the human organism and have no objective status at all.

In this field, we are beyond the data which the tools of empirical method can handle with a high degree of accuracy. With some certainty we may distinguish many of the obvious projections of the imagination, but we cannot discern the significance of many of the data. Yet these data are real, meaningful, and relevant to religious living. They point to the numinous, the holy, the awesome, to which people respond with fear as much as with faith. Some account must be made of their presence. They point to a mystery which can be shown but cannot be explained. They cannot be accepted uncritically on the authority of the one who has the experience, and yet they cannot be summarily dismissed.

It is for these reasons that an empirical theology must have a superstructure. This superstructure is not the revealed theology of the orthodox tradition, although tradition may contribute richly to it. It is, rather, the groping of the human mind to interpret the revealed truths of God which have come through human experience, especially through persons of superlative insight. Even here, however, we have to start with the data of experience as far as we can reconstruct them, and then apply our creative imaginations to the task. Even in the case of Jesus, for example, we need to distinguish between his limitations as a first-century Jew and his insights into the nature of God; between the occasional and the permanent in his teachings; between the traditional view of his death and resurrection and the renderings that do more justice to the facts as we can reconstruct them.

Therefore, we must have an adequate method for the building of a superstructure for our basic theology based on experience. This involves an adequate value theory, a means for interpreting myth, poetry, symbol and other forms of religious language, and a satisfactory system of analogy and models, whereby those deeper experiences may be translated into the common experiences of everyday life.

If God can be found in values, and in the process which brings them into existence, we need a sound theory of what values are. Values are relations between things. They are appreciable activities relating parts of the actual world. We say a certain thing is good because it is something which can be appreciated by us. A sirloin steak is good in itself because it is appreciable, and we can verify this fact by eating the steak and judging the consequences. The value depends upon a series of relations involving the steak which make it appreciable and finally upon our relation to the steak for verification. The same thing is true of any particular good, whether it be money, a symphony concert, love in the family, a new car, or getting rid of rubbish. These are all values, because of the appreciable relations which are set up.

These values are part of the processes of living, and thus we can observe them. From this point of view, we may claim that the processes by which and through which values come into being are the work of God. It is in this sense that Douglas Clyde Macintosh spoke of God as "the divine value-producing factor" and Henry Nelson Wieman referred to God as "the growth of meaning and value in the world." We are able to cooperate with these value-producing forces to bring about the creation of new values and to conserve the traditional ones. This is a fact of experience which can be verified. When values are conceived in this way, they enter into the heart of empirical theology, for God is conceived both as sustaining power and as producer of values.

Value judgments also form part of the superstructure of theology. We rely on our concepts of the highest values in order to sense the moral grandeur of God. God *ought* to be at least what our finest and most sensitive minds can conceive, although there is always the assurance that God is more than that. God *ought* to be good, intelligent, and personal in some sense analogous to human experience of these qualities, although such claims may not be taken literally. But even to argue from the *ought* to the *is* is dangerous, and to do it by means of analogy may provide illumination at the expense of reality. Such thinking opens a wedge to wishful thinking and psychological projection, and this can be fatal. But if value judgments are conceived in terms of actual and potential activities, and if value judgments are consistent with what can be observed, we have a tool for gaining additional insight into the nature of deity.[2]

Another means of extending the system of beliefs is by analysis of myth. Myth is understood as a means of stating truths in a certain imaginative way because no simple, logical statement carries the full meaning of the reflected experience. Like legend, folktale, or poetry, it has both intelligent and affective power in making communication possible. The myth of creation in Genesis tells us something significant about the nature of God and God's relation to humanity, although when taken literally it is atrocious both as theology and as science. Many of the legends surrounding the

2. For a critical analysis of the use of judgments about value, see my *The American Spirit in Theology* (Philadelphia: Pilgrim Press, 1974), pp. 126–129.

birth, life, and resurrection of Jesus aid us in evaluating his character and his work, no matter how incredulous we may be about such stories when taken as literal fact. Providing we place them in the right language category and know which game of communication we are playing, we can appropriate the religious value of such stories.[3]

Poetry is also a form of religious expression. Dante's *Inferno* as poetry gives us insight into the nature of God's judgment and into human moral responsibility, but when it was taken literally it set back theology for centuries. Religious poetry may be bad theology and often sinks into sentimentality, as any hymnal abundantly illustrates, but even bad hymns illustrate the emotive power of poetry wed to music. The hymns of the church and its poetry have done much to arouse religious emotions to respond to the love of God when a dry-as-dust theological tome leaves people asking for nourishment—for bread rather than stones. Poetry gives concrete imagery to religious truths, but it must be used critically as well as appreciatively. It both stimulates and provides insights into the nature of God so that the response may be in terms of genuine ethical behavior.

Symbols are important for the expression of religious truth. Protestantism has lost much because it has ignored many traditional symbols. On the other hand, many symbols have lost their power to communicate and therefore serve no useful purpose. Symbols are simply shortcuts for the representation of religious truths, and, providing they point to realities, they are valid additions to the foundations of theology. Symbols, like myth and poetry, are endangered when they are taken literally, but as pictorial or verbal representations they have deep religious value. Creedal denominations, especially, must take every precaution to protect the symbolic character of their affirmations of faith. Even when a critical investigation shows that creeds are based on bad science,

3. See my *The Language Gap and God* (Philadelphia: United Church Press, 1970), esp. pp. 62–76.

confused theology, and an outmoded view of Scripture, they may serve as affirmations of loyalty. Horace Bushnell saw this clearly when he said that he would gladly subscribe to any number of creeds, for he was sure that each one contained some aspect of truth.

Symbols are more than signs. Signs only point, but to some degree symbols also show the reality for which they stand. This result, I presume, is primarily subjective and is due to some kind of association with the reality behind the symbol. Therefore, symbols can lose their power. However, symbols cannot be invented or discarded at will, as there is a strong cultural factor that determines both their power and their failure. The problem today with symbols derived from previous cultures is to determine to what extent their power continues to operate. In a technological society dominated by scientific symbols, we need to examine carefully the inherited symbols in order to understand whether they can continue to be useful and to evaluate emerging symbols that may serve in the present or future.

## THEOLOGY AND ANALOGY

The purposes of theology are to establish the truth of religious beliefs and to communicate those beliefs. Communication is never the sharing of identical ideas, nor is communication complete unless it points to a similar experience for the other. By the use of words, gestures, symbols, and the like, communication evokes a similar experience in the one who receives the communication. Only this is not always the case. Attempts at communication may evoke an experience diametrically opposed to the one desired, or it may result in no experience at all. It is for this reason that a sound knowledge of the method of analogy is important.

The method of analogy is to appeal to an experience which is sufficiently common that it may be transferred to another realm of experience without altering the concept. This must be done consciously, for when an analogy is taken literally it becomes crystallized and distorted and loses its force. Analogies are important in all forms of communication but are essential for pointing to the essential mystery at the center of religious belief and behavior. When we speak of God as Father, Shepherd, Person, Mind, Earth Mother, Lion of Judah, Creator, and in so many other ways, we are using analogies that may help to understand something of the nature of God, or at least to address God as one who is a creative and transforming power. 1926853

Analogy is supplemented by symbols, poetry, myths, and various types of imagery. These ways of thinking are never literally accurate, but they evoke representations of reality for human minds. They must be open to the most rigorous criticism, and they must stand for truth rather than for the stimulation of the emotions, although they have great emotive power. Such supplements to the beliefs based on a rigorous empiricism must be used carefully, but only in such ways can we go beyond where empiricism points. In communicating our beliefs, only such methods are likely to lead to the disclosures that we intend.

Metaphor is a form of analogy. Metaphors arise in the imagination as we see the connection between secular and sacred images. They are "rooted in disclosures and born in insight."[4] When we say that "God is light," for example, we bring together two realms that carry their own mystery and yet illuminate the meaning of both. Thus metaphor can become a way both of achieving insight and of communicating it, especially when a series of metaphors is used. But there must be some degree of consistency among the metaphors or the result will be confused and chaotic.

Models are helpful in thinking and talking about religious beliefs. In designing a new automobile, a literal model of an experimental car may be used. But in religion, models are *never* literal. They draw their meaning from analogy, metaphor, and even useful fic-

---

4. Ian T. Ramsey, *Models and Mystery* (London: Oxford University Press, 1964), p. 50.

tions. They serve as the basis for the development of new theories or as the expression of attitudes, such as awe, reverence, and moral obligation. They are nonliteral ways of interpreting experience and they have a power that more formal beliefs sometimes lack. These models must fit into one's overall view of things or paradigm in order to provide coherence and consistency.

Many types of models have been used for the portrayal of God, and the obsolescence of some of these is one of the reasons for the crisis of belief today. The monarchial model of God as omnipotent king who determines every event in advance and is therefore responsible for evil and suffering, with the result that human freedom is denied, is obsolete for many. So is the model of the divine clockmaker. The personal or agent model has many adherents still, but is under fire in many quarters. A *process model*, which suggests that God is unsurpassed but not absolute, at least in the working of God in the world, may be a suitable model for today. When this is supplemented by a model drawn from the work of Jesus as the Christ, Christians may find that their model for God is not only believable but also supportive of their profoundest religious attitudes and commitments.[5]

All of this is to say that there is a vision which cannot be completely captured by any system of analogies, metaphors, or models, for the vision points to an ultimate mystery. But by the revision of our beliefs in terms of careful use of analogies, metaphors, and models which are consistent with experience, we may become more at home in the universe. We cannot settle for sloppy thinking, sentimentality, and undue reliance on previous thought. We need to go beyond the transient experiences which lack significance and to examine those which point us toward the mystery that stands over and yet within our lives.

God is in experience and beyond experience. Unless God is in the world, God is inaccessible. In religious living, we experience both

5. See Ian G. Barbour, *Myths, Models, and Paradigms* (New York: Harper & Row, 1974), pp. 49–70, 165–170.

the nearness and the majestic otherness of God, which lead to models of the mysterious and the holy. We may face God as an enemy, we may seek for God and find the void, or we may discover a companion whose nature is persuasive and transforming love. Our imaginations are fed by the hidden nature of God, and some of our most profound images may never be fully accounted for by empirical method.

God comes into our experience, so that those who have eyes to see may say, "Look! There is God!" And then others will see, too; but some will mock and say that it is just an hallucination. Especially when it is a private experience, we find difficulty in sharing, and yet what happens to us in our solitariness needs to be shared with the community of believers. For some of us, there are intimations of such experiences and we fail to recognize them as such until we are spoken to by another who can articulate what we dimly discern. Perhaps what we need is a more relevant imagery, a better analogy, a model derived from another area of experience, or a whole new paradigm. Faulty theologies and negative evaluations of experience have hindered our ability to understand the religious dimension of experience.

Yet there is Jesus, and the life he lived and the experience of him by the disciples led the early Christian community to ascribe these words to Jesus: "Whoever has seen me has seen the Father" (Jn 14:9,G). In the experience of many persons since then, these words have been seen as true, and the incarnation has been the central theme of Christian living and belief. People do come to God without Jesus, as did the prophets and many since then in various religious traditions, but for Christians the way has been through faith in Jesus Christ. The early Christian community was so convinced of this that they said that no person could come to God except through Christ, and this became a firm conviction of the Christian Church.

This emphasis on experience can become unbalanced if it is not controlled by critical analysis and imagination. Private experiences and those of isolated groups need always to be checked against the common experiences of society. It is here that the twentieth-century person, trained in modern science and technology, will be critical of many historical formulations even when seen as proper analogies or metaphors. This kind of criticism will also operate in the realm of myth and symbol, so that a kind of emotional impoverishment may result; this is a risk we have to take, for religious truth cannot be compromised for subjective reasons. But empiricism does not tell the whole story, and therefore we turn to supplementary methods and make full use of the creative imagination and metaphysics in order to provide a way of looking on the universe with God at the center.

The methods described so briefly in this chapter need to be worked out in detail by competent theologians. But the scientific, religious, and appreciative spirit which is seen as adequately critical and constructive can be applied by all who seek to believe on their own terms. The remainder of this book develops such a method as applied to Christian beliefs, as seen by one whose own biases were described in the opening chapter, and the reader therefore has a basis for comparison and evaluation as the argument develops.

# 3
# *What God Does*

When we ask if there is a God, we expect to have some kind of evidence for either a yes or a no. That evidence, we have suggested, begins with the analysis of human experience, including relationships both external and internal, and reflection upon it. The problem is to discover what processes are in the world, society, and personal experience to which the concept of deity can be applied. We cannot start with a preconceived idea of what God must be, although we need a theory about the nature of God that can be tested. It is not a question of the kind of divinity we want or need, but of what processes act to sustain and transform us. Our task is to observe the world in which we live, to discover what activities may be ascribed to God, and then to seek for a concept which best describes the functions we have discovered. We can probably start with no preconceived notions, although we need a modicum of theory in order to know what we are looking for, and we do have a wealth of inherited experience and tradition upon which we can draw. We can be our own theologians, but we will be wiser ones if we take account of the history of ideas and of the variety of views open to us today. As in all fields of knowledge, there are experts in the area of religion who know more than we do, and we should rely on their findings and theories as we develop our own beliefs.

Our approach to the nature of God is reducible to three main divisions: (1) In this chapter, we ask the question, "How does God work?" (2) In the following chapter, we ask, "Who is God in the light of how God works?" and (3) "How can God be understood through analogy, symbol, story, model, and imagery?"

If God be real, we must first seek the reality or process which gives us knowledge of God's working. All knowledge is based upon those processes which function in the world of human experience. Such experience may conveniently be subdivided into the realm of nature, the areas of human and social relations, and the effects on human personality. We must look into each of these realms to discover how God works.

## THE REALM OF NATURE

The theologian can never again be an expert in the field of cosmology. The cosmos is too large and complex for any theory competently to explain it, and no one mind can comprehend or develop an adequate world view. The scientist and the philosopher suffer from the same disability as the theologian. Each person works in a specialized field, and it is from the perspective of that field that one must necessarily view the cosmos. This means that every expert has prejudices, limitations, and insights which are brought to the problem at hand. At the same time, some attempt can be made in forming a composite picture of the world based upon the findings of scientists and philosophers, and the theologian can say that within certain limits processes can be observed which seem to reveal the presence of God.

The cosmos is interpreted as an organism of closely interrelated processes. The human person is a very small entity in this organism, but at the same time the human being is a complex organism on a much smaller scale who constantly mystifies the biologist, psychologist, and sociologist. A person is in a constant process of becoming and perishing, and yet what perishes is not lost but becomes the basis for future becoming. The greatness of the universe is reflected in the knowledge acquired over many centuries by human beings.

The cosmic organism, as observed and interpreted by human beings, has a high degree of consistency. There is some degree of relationship between the activities of the cosmos and the purposes of human beings. There are certain dependable relations in the world which guarantee that experiments performed under similar conditions will produce identical results. When an experiment is repeated a sufficient number of times, we say that there is a "natural law" which covers these activities. All sciences have such presuppositions. The universe is dependable because it "obeys" such laws. These laws are descriptions by the human mind of the behavior under observation, and anyone can observe the functions of various aspects of nature and understand that they do follow such laws.

If the cosmos is consistent, there must be a reason for it. However, there are some complicating factors. The universe is not wholly predictable. There is evidence of the emergence of novelty at all levels of existence. The principle of indeterminacy indicates that minute entities are unpredictable. Chance and freedom seem to play some part in the processes we observe. This leads to a deeper richness in terms of surprising events, but it also challenges us to a more complex overview of the nature of reality.

One possible explanation is that chance is the primary factor. No overall purpose or even partial direction can be discerned. Many people are satisfied with this explanation. Certainly there are events which, in the light of all of our predictions, seem to be due to chance. When chance is the basic hypothesis, however, it fails to account for the evidence that statistically this world could not have happened on that theory. But here we are! Why is this particular planet at the proper temperature to support and sustain human life? Not only the temperature, but the things we eat, the water we drink, the coal we mine, and the material for the clothes we wear, among many items, are just right to make possible human life. The emergence of human consciousness operating in terms of rational principles and adjusting to the conditions for living meaningfully is difficult to account for according to the principle of chance. Surely this is not a satisfactory explanation.

Because chance is an inadequate hypothesis, many people suggest an alternative. Many scientists and philosophers argue that only if the cosmos was created by a divine mind with a definite and fixed purpose could this world have come into existence. God is the great purposer beneath the surface of human events, and controls the future as well. For many people this is the solution. However, if we rely on the method of interpreting what we actually can observe, this hypothesis claims too much. If God is the creator, the world was created long before there were people to observe it. Our most competent scientists cannot tell us much about the origin of the world, and they disagree about the beginnings of the human species. It *may* be true that God is the creator, but we cannot prove what cannot be observed. It is a possible hypothesis, and if it is the only alternative to the proposition that all was created by chance, we are likely to take it.

For some, however, there is another choice. There must be a reason that nature is dependable. Neither chance nor a creator can be shown conclusively to be the reason. When we look at nature itself, another possibility is opened to us. There is, within nature as we observe it, evidence of a *creative order* which sustains and promotes the cosmos. It may be a plurality of processes which are working to bring about the integration of the natural organism, or it may be a single process working within nature. It is this creative order, a principle or structure or process of integration, which brings about our orderly universe.

This can be observed in every science. The biologist sees it in the growth of a child, the psychologist in the organizing power of the brain, the chemist in the reactions of elements in a test tube, the sociologist in the relations between human beings, the astronomer in the stars. If all life is flux, it is no wonder that the physicists are becoming convinced that ultimate reality is not matter but energy or spirit.

This process of integration in nature is not to be identified with inevitable progress. It is obvious that humanity has suffered throwbacks, that nature can take turns that seem to be of negative value, that there can be mutations that are totally unexpected. I had a teacher of philosophy who maintained that the dinosaur was evidence of God's sense of humor. But it is also clear to many people that there are increasing interrelationships that seem to be good in the realm of nature. The universe is an organism, and there is growth within it, but there is no inevitable progress. Whatever processes guide or determine the direction of the universe are guiding it toward closer connections.

In this process, values have emerged. If values are objective relations between events, they also can be observed. They are appreciable activities which do not depend on human beings for either their existence or their appreciation. They are just as much in the external world as that which can be measured. The Grand Canyon is beautiful whether or not there is anyone there to appreciate it. Values and the potentiality of being appreciated appear on the human scene because of the nature of reality. We may say that there is a "value producing factor" in the universe, and we can observe "the growth of meaning and value in the world."[1]

Nature is so constructed that it may best be conceived as an organism, in which we can see at work the processes which guarantee the dependableness of nature and the emergence of values. We may use the model of the human body, with all of its interrelated parts functioning together as a unity. The problem is whether these processes are open to religious interpretation. We have already indicated that some people are content to interpret all that happens as due to blind chance, and although this is highly improbable, it is a scientifically respectable hypothesis. Others take a religiously traditional position, claiming that belief in a purposive, personal God who is the creator and director of the cosmos is the

1. These phrases belong to D. C. Macintosh and H. N. Wieman, respectively.

most likely conclusion. Certainly this cannot be ruled out as inadmissable. The third position is not inconsistent with the second, but does not claim so much. According to this view, these processes are viewed as the work of God in the world, and therefore they give us valuable data concerning the nature of God. God works through the cosmos to bring about closer relationships, the growth of value, and the emergence of new elements. There is room in this view for the presence of genuine chance and the emergence of novelty, and therefore the future is open. Whatever the ultimate relationship may be between God and the world, this much may be claimed with practical certainty. God is at work in our midst, achieving these things, and we can see the wonders which God has wrought.

### HUMAN SOCIETY AND HISTORY

Philosophers are inclined to examine the problem of God at work in nature; empirically minded theologians are concerned with God's presence in experience and especially in religious experience; traditionally oriented theologians have found most of their evidence in the examination of history and especially of biblical history; but God's activity in human society and social relations has been less frequently examined, especially when social and political action is in question.

We need to consider seriously how we can discover processes in history which provide evidence for our interpretation of the nature of God. The whole story of the Jewish Scriptures focused on what God does for the chosen people. Although the way in which God is interpreted in the Old Testament is often primitive and anthropomorphic, the evidence in terms of moral and spiritual values in relation to corporate experience is central to any understanding of either Judaism or Christianity today.

The prophets saw God in history, working through judgment and requiring righteousness. When people and nations constantly ignore the laws of morality, there are consequences which can be predicted. These laws of morality seem to be statistical, just as are laws determined by the natural sciences, and there is a similar reliability. When persons act in one way or another consistently, there will be predictable results. The difficulties in the economic system which lead to business depressions, dislocation of political processes, and undue suffering from poverty and often starvation can be seen in biblical or moral terms as due to human greed, selfishness, dishonesty, and love of power. Instead of seeking rewards for efforts backed by love and service of others, there is the desire to get something for nothing. The problems of economic cycles and political catastrophes are more complex than this, but when economic and social rules are disregarded, so are moral rules. The result is social injustice leading to undue suffering. The prophet Amos saw this many years ago when he talked about selling "the needy for a pair of shoes" (Amos 2:6 RSV). The religious interpretation of God at work in history points to a demand for more sound relationships, based on social morality, as a foundation for hope for the future.

There is also a positive side about the working of God in history and in society. There are social processes which bring about increase of values. Sometimes there is growth of interpersonal, social, and political relationships which are not necessarily desired, and out of such unexpected relationships new and unpredictable values may emerge. The economic process, for example, sets up connections which make for possible closer relations, and in spite of all the conflicts which occur there is increase of goods. The abundance is there, even if we fail to take advantage of it. The connections provided by the economic process are a firm reality which we may ignore, but the risk is great. There are ways of working through such processes to provide for greater sharing and a greater degree of social justice.

Christianity has always interpreted God as at work in society and history. The incarnation finds its meaning in the events surrounding the work of Jesus, and we learn about God's nature as a result of the movement of redemption which is centered in Jesus

Christ. The key to God's work in history as both persuasive love and righteous judgment lies in the revelation which comes through the impact of Jesus on history. The power of God to reach people and nations is still mediated through the capacity of Jesus Christ to attract us to a loving God.

The processes of history and human society are realities of everyday experience. Too often we have failed to be sensitive to the working of God through these processes. God pervades society and is present in all that is just and ordered, but when God's will is thwarted the resistance is evidenced through wars, depressions, and other human catastrophes. All the processes of society and history are not God's work, but God is in our midst, and by observing how God functions we come to an understanding of God's presence in farm and city, slum and suburb, and in politics and the international order.

## PERSONAL EXPERIENCE

God, then, is at the least a creative power which brings about the structure of reality and the emergence of values. These are processes that can be observed as external to the self. But religion is never simply observation and its interpretation, and a God who works in these ways seems remote from our personal needs and interests. It is claimed that God also works in and through the individual, and it is this type of experience which provides the data for the final test of belief in God.

Douglas C. Macintosh claimed that there is a dependable right religious adjustment which every person can make. It begins with a sense of yearning or aspiration which is followed by the experience of the presence of something other than ourselves, and this leads to a specific commitment to that reality in an act which is both moral and spiritual. This may lead to a definite change in the direction of one's purposes, or it may result in a deeper devotion in the same direction as before. It may give strength and courage to overcome obstacles in the self and beyond, or it may give comfort and patience to accept the inevitable, and often it is a combination of both.[2] "Do not be conformed to this world but be transformed by the renewal of your mind, that you may prove what is the will of God, what is good and acceptable and perfect" (Rom. 12:2, RSV). God is the power which is the source of experiences of transformation.

There are many case studies of experiences of this type, ranging from the extreme and sometimes morbid ones recounted by William James in *The Varieties of Religious Experience* to the normal confrontation with God which is part of everyone's life whether recognized as such or not. It is not a peculiarly Christian experience but appears in the records of all religions in one form or another. It is this attention to other religions which strengthens the universality of the claim that religious experience in some form is possible for every person in every culture.

> Seek the LORD while he may be found,
>     call upon him while he is near
> let the wicked forsake his way,
>     and the unrighteous man his thoughts;
> let him return to the LORD, that he may have
>     mercy on him,
> and to our God, for he will abundantly
>     pardon (Is. 55:6–7, RSV).

The confidence that one can be restored to a right relationship with God, that one's conduct and commitment will be transformed, and that all this will lead to some degree of beatitude seems to be common to most religious claims.

These experiences may not be of the mystical type, although some claim that there are degrees of mysticism all the way from a sense of union with the absolute to what James called a "mystical

2. D. C. Macintosh, ed., *Religious Realism* (New York: Macmillan, 1931), p. 323.

germ." Meditation, contemplation, prayer, devotional reading of Scriptures and other literature, music, art, and ethical decision-making or problem-solving are all likely to have religious effects. There are corporate experiences that parallel these and yet have the added impetus of social support and meaning, especially in terms of symbolic forms and rituals. In all these and some other experiences, it can be said that God is acting as a sustaining power which stimulates the human organism to endeavors of higher values than normally would be expected. If the experience is valid, we can know it by its fruits.

All who claim to have such experiences do not show it in their lives. There are always those who can be converted every Sunday and steal again every Monday. These experiences are recognized as false by every observer. There are also those who claim to be on the side of righteousness and do not demonstrate it by their actions. Much of the disillusionment with institutional religion results from the avoidance of behavior necessary to meet human needs by both leaders and followers when significant human values are at stake.

Yet, as Whitehead has said, "the power of God is the worship he inspires."[3] These experiences are not purely subjective, even though they operate in what James called the "subliminal" realm. There is a stability about our religious searchings, and we become convinced that God can be trusted to act consistently as persuasive love, and that God's transforming power is available to us at all times. We cannot reduce this evidence to statistical laws, for it is more like our model of personal relations where trust and response are factors.

This is no easy optimism, for religious experience is "the transition from God the void to God the enemy, and from God the enemy to God the companion," according to Whitehead.[4] By this, he means that the results of religion may be evil rather than good and that destruction rather than transformation may be the end.

3. Alfred North Whitehead, *Science and the Modern World* (New York: Macmillan, 1925), p. 276.
4. Alfred N. Whitehead, *Religion in the Making* (New York: Macmillan, 1926), pp. 16–17.

The significant thing about religion is not its "necessary goodness" but "its transcendent importance."[5] Psychologically, there are situations where depth experiences lead to a disarrangement or breakdown of one's personality, so that the person becomes incompetent to participate in social relations, or develops complexes of persecution, or uses religious motivation for immoral activities.

When one has a solitary experience, it is important that there be a return to the believing community for a common verification. Sometimes this is not forthcoming, because the experience has been hallucinatory or a vision leading to inacceptable behavior or to irrational thoughts, and the wider wisdom of the group is able to provide correction or a new direction. It is always possible, however, that the solitary experience is valid and that the group is in error, for otherwise the church would not have a record of stoning its prophets. What is needed in empirical theology is a supporting community of those who take seriously the empirical method, much as described by Charles Sanders Peirce, for then there may be a consensus leading to verification. There may still be differences in interpretation of the data, but if the data are established, the first step toward verification has been taken.

As we reflect on religious experience, we may interpret the process working through us as creativity or the creative order. To verify this, there are certain results to look for. (1) A new perspective comes from interrelations with other individuals and groups that leads to an increase of qualitative meaning and new values in our lives, so that our range of knowing and valuing is expanded. (2) Our various perspectives are brought together, resulting in an expanding range and depth of mutually sustaining activities, as our values are modified and then integrated into our existing value structure. (3) Our appreciable world is seen in a broader perspective, especially when there is a moment of new disclosure in an extraordinary experience. (4) We experience a growth of the sense of

5. Ibid., p. 18.

community as interpersonal relationships are transformed and deepened. These four events are so locked together that they are seen as a single process of creativity.[6] God is experienced no longer as void or enemy but as companion.

There is a religious dimension in all experience, so that we are not limited to those experiences which are traditionally called "religious." Our experiences of nature and history as well as our interpersonal and solitary experiences provide evidence that we need to consider. As we turn to the concept of God that results from an examination of the evidence within the paradigm of process thinking, we will be seeking what Ian T. Ramsey called "empirical fit" or "empirical accord." The problem is to decide what beliefs fit the evidence well enough and to base our religious living on sound thinking, so that we will be led to align our purpose with God's aims in the world.

For Christians, the supreme example of what God does in and through human beings is the life of Jesus of Nazareth. For him God was no illusion, no subjective intuition. God was a living presence, who responded to every act of devotion with an outpouring of love. Jesus felt this love, and he used the model of Father to describe what God is like. God was universally present to those who sought God, and God's love, mercy, and justice sustained Jesus in his ministry, and later on his disciples were supported in their work of announcing the coming of the kingdom and the forming of the church. It may be said that God worked through Jesus in a unique way, but throughout the ages the saints of Christendom have felt the same presence and have sought the same kingdom. This kind of evidence is available through the Christian tradition and is not to be taken lightly.

God's work is to be discovered wherever people turn. Strictly speaking, we do not see God except within an aura of mystery. We see God's handiwork in the processes of daily living, whether it be

6. See Henry Nelson Wieman, *The Source of Human Good* (Chicago: University of Chicago Press, 1946; Southern Illinois University Press, 1964), pp. 58–69.

in nature, in society and history, or in personal experience. There is an "empirical anchor" in our common worship which tends to verify our God-talk. By our observations of what God does, we may formulate beliefs of who God is.

# 4
# *Who Is God?*

When we begin to understand how God works as a process of integration, as a principle which supplies structure to the natural, social, historical, moral, and spiritual orders, and as that power which sustains and transforms human beings in their spiritual quest for full lives, we have the basic data which provide the clues for our understanding of God's nature. In order to answer the question of who God is, we must first present a rigorous, limited, empirical description based on what our findings seem to prove. Then we can use our minimum description of God as the foundation for exploring other possibilities, bringing us to the realm which William James called "overbeliefs." These latter may be just as true as our more empirical description, but they take us into other categories of language where we cannot make the same kind of empirical tests.

### Empirical Findings

In one sense, God *is* what God *does*, and therefore we may describe God as "the growth of meaning and value in the world." But God is more than what we see done, and we may call God the *factor* in the world which is the source and producer of values. God then is what is behind the growth of value, just as people are not only what they do but are also the conscious minds and organisms which are the source of activity.

It has been suggested that *God* is not really a noun but a verb. If this is one way of thinking about God, we need to consider the data in terms of process rather than substance, just as we consider a person as an organism rather than a static reality. But we still have to ask what is the continuing focus in the process by which we can identify it. If, among other possibilities, God is that process by which we are transformed, strengthened, directed, comforted, forgiven, saved, and which lures us into feelings of wonder, awe, and reverence, we find ourselves stretching for descriptions which take us beyond the implications of "the growth of meaning and value" or "creative process."

As far as empirical verification is concerned, however, the data do not point much beyond this with any certainty. But if this much is verified, we have a starting point for our theologizing. At least we are talking about a deity which exists, about a process in the universe which brings about the existence of values in a dependable and predictable manner. We do not know all the conditions for cooperation with God, but we know that God works in these ways. We know that this factor, which we call God, works independently of human purposes and actions, and to that extent at least is transcendent. Chiefly, however, we know God as immanent in what is going on in the world.

Daniel Day Williams suggested that Henry Nelson Wieman, whose empirical approach stressed this view of God as "creative event," "actually stated what has become the practice of people in wide areas of our culture, including much of the practice in established religious institutions. When we ask what [people] actually put their trust in as revealed by their actions, we see that we may require something like 'creative interchange' to describe the operative process to which we give our attention and even our devotion."[1] This is a significant observation, and perhaps it may be

1. Daniel Day Williams, in William S. Minor, ed., *Charles Hartshorne and Henry Nelson Wieman* (Carbondale, Illinois: Foundation for Creative Philosophy, 1969), p. 56.

helpful if we look at some of our religious practices and assumptions on these terms. But most of us will not be satisfied to stop at this point in our own creative thinking and imaginative reconstruction.

### OVERBELIEFS

The findings of a strictly empirical method do not tell the whole story. They provide an introduction to the concept of God, but the result is a kind of vagueness and abstraction that needs more concrete imagery. This is necessary not only to meet the needs of the religious imagination but also to fill out the picture of God within our world view. For many of us, it would be absurd to pray to the "creative interaction" or say, "O Principle of Concretion." Our deity may well be these things, just as a particular organism may be described as a chemical or biological process rather than as our friend named John Jones. We need auxiliary methods in order to clothe the nakedness of our original concept. Such inferences are valid insofar as they are consistent with the findings of experience.

Many suggestions come from tradition and the Bible. God has been thought of as loving, good, intelligent, and personal. Usually God has been pictured as the creator or first cause, and sometimes as the creative order, who is in control of the happenings in a world of discord and strife, and who knows what our ultimate destiny is. Already we are in the realm of analogy and speculation about what is ultimately a mystery. We have taken terms which are meaningful in human relationships and applied them to deity. We have moved from one language category to another.

When pronouns are used to refer to God, they are usually masculine. Yet there are feminine terms for God. Wisdom is a frequent synonym for God or the Word. And Wisdom is feminine.

To him who is without sense she says,
"Come, eat of my bread
    and drink of the wine I have mixed,
Leave simpleness, and live,
    and walk in the way of insight" (Prov. 9:4a–6,RSV).

Wisdom protected the first-formed father of the
world, when he alone had been created;
    she delivered him from his transgression,
and gave him strength to rule all things (Wis. Sol. 10:1–2,RSV).

Or compare the Logos becoming flesh or the son coming from the
Father with this:

The Lord himself created wisdom;
    he saw her and apportioned her,
    he poured her out upon all his works.
She dwells with all flesh according to his gift,
    and he supplied her to those who love him (Sir. 1:9–10, RSV).

Jesus used the female imagery of the hen in expressing his concern for the holy city: "O Jerusalem, Jerusalem, the city that
murders the prophets and stones the messengers sent to her! How
often have I longed to gather your children, as a hen gathers her
brood under her wings; but you would not let me" (Mt. 23:27,
NEB). Furthermore, the original Hebrew for spirit, *ruach*, is
feminine, which suggests that we might use the pronoun "she" for
all references to the Holy Spirit.[2]

The problem of gender is due to the limitations of language, for it
is clear that God has neither human nor sexual characteristics. Yet,

2. See Letty Russell, *Human Liberation in a Feminist Perspective—A
Theology* (Philadelphia: Westminster Press, 1974), pp. 97–103.

because God is an entity who responds in some ways to personal address and who enters into interpersonal relations, it is difficult to use the pronoun *it*. *He*, *she*, and *it* are all unsatisfactory. We can use pronouns only when we are addressing God, when we say "you" or "thou."

We seek to speak of God by name. Yet the Hebrew tradition that God's name is too holy to be pronounced led them to substitute *Lord* for *Yahweh*. The Bible does provide some names, such as Father, King, Lord, Most High, Almighty, Counselor, Guiding Light, the Eternal. When Moses wanted to know God's name, God said, "I am who I am." And then God added that the name is Yahweh (Ex. 3:14,15).

We may talk about God by using analogies, metaphors, and models. We *construe* God *as* love; or we *see* God *as* good; or we *experience* God *as* just and righteous; or we *interpret* God *as* personal. These statements are not strictly synonymous, but they point to our way of speaking about God, and we respond as creatures to the giver of life in a variety of ways.

We think of God *as* holy. Our experiences of the numinous, whether in terms of Rudolf Otto's idea of the holy or in terms of aesthetic awareness, point beyond ourselves to that which arouses in us feelings of awe, wonder, and reverence. There is mystery, in the sense of something incomprehensible rather than something waiting to be solved, which is a religious dimension of much of our experience. The implications of this type of experience lead us to think of God as transcendent or superhuman or beyond the human realm. Yet often this experience is in terms of a feeling of union with God or at least of some degree of intimate communion; so that we say that God is immanent as well as transcendent. This is probably the origin of what has been called supernaturalism, but transcendence can be thought of within the organic wholeness of process thinking.

We construe God *as* love or *as* loving. There is much in the tradition to support this view, especially in the teachings of Jesus. God is thought of as an individual, as an actual entity, or as a series of activities, and therefore in relation with humanity. If God's aim is to be loving, this means that God is willing to grant freedom to others, and to take the consequences of that freedom. These consequences lead to suffering, to accepting the tragic in human experience, to bearing our loss and failure, and to transmuting this suffering and failure into something positive. God suffers and therefore is changed by what we do, as far as God's relationships are concerned; but there is a sense in which God's everlastingness protects the invulnerability of sovereign rule, so that God's integrity is not threatened.[3] "God is the great companion—the fellow-sufferer who understands," as Whitehead put it.[4]

If God is loving, there is a question of whether God coerces us. The emphasis in this approach is on persuasion, so that freedom may be considered genuine. But persuasion has power, and the difference between persuasion and coercion is a matter of degree. John Oman spoke of God's "persuasive grace" as distinguished from "irresistable grace,"[5] and this seems more in keeping with the meaning of love. If God has the power to take the impact of human suffering and sin and to transform it, we see the basis for love as forgiveness; for God restores broken relationships through reconciliation.

Our observation of God's working is centered on the increase of good in the world. What we call God's action is seen *as if* it is good in every conceivable situation, and therefore it is reasonable to conclude that God is good. There is a sense in which God's goodness is imposed on the world, for we do not equate God's goodness with human goodness. Wherever we observe the growth of good, we assume that God is involved as the source of that goodness. God's aim for us is thought of in terms of a goodness that transcends human aims. When our relationship with God is sound, the benefits to us are good. But there is evil in the world, and we must

3. See Daniel Day Williams, *The Spirit and Forms of Love* (New York: Harper & Row, 1968), pp. 122–129.

4. Alfred North Whitehead, *Process and Reality* (New York: Macmillan, 1929), p. 532.

5. *Grace and Personality* (Cambridge: Cambridge University Press, 1917).

decide whether to place responsibility for evil on God or come to some other understanding of the causes of evil.

We come to a similar conclusion concerning justice. There seems to be a stern justice in the world. The farmer prays for rain, and it does rain—in the Atlantic Ocean. He harvests his crops and dries his fruits, and he gets hailstorms in July. Insofar as God is the source of natural phenomena through the creativity that we ascribe to God, we see no partiality. But the same impartiality runs through human relationships. Was not Jesus crucified? Are not the righteous everywhere persecuted for his sake? This model of impartiality is significant, even though it is obvious that rainstorms are not due to particular decisions of an erratic will of God.

If God plays no favorites on the negative side, it is equally evident that God's blessings are for all. In the long run, the justice of God shows itself superior to the judgments of human beings. It is a rough justice that causes nations to fall, economic systems to break down, and civilizations to perish, but the judgment of God falls on sinful nations through perfectly natural channels. We may hope that in the end those who seek to align themselves with God's aims are justified, even though in the process of becoming and perishing this is not always immediately evident. God is aligned with human righteousness, even though for a time the wicked conquer; this does not mean that "God is on our side" but rather that human beings have discerned what it means to be fully human in God's sight.

Justice is always tempered with mercy. God forgives us even when we know not what we do. "If you forgive others when they offend you, your heavenly Father will forgive you, too" (Mt. 6:14,G). God does forgive those who turn to God and who seek to love their neighbors as themselves. God's stern and seemingly crude justice is mixed with a specific and forgiving love which passes understanding. Justice is applied according to the laws of God to groups and individuals. It might be called almost wholesale in its application. God's love is also according to law, but it is retail in its application, so that even those who are suffering under the judgment of God may, *at the same time*, be recipients of God's healing love. Thus, in the face of God's judgment upon a sinful generation, we may come into God's healing presence and be given the strength to overcome hatred, suffering, and tragedy. The redemptive power of God's love is always mixed with judgment, so that we are brought to our knees before God in confession and repentance and therefore become aware of God's forgiving and reconciling love.

The only way to account for such experiences of love mixed with justice is to look on God *as* intelligent. Again, we are working within the limitations of a human model and must not take the analogy literally. If the only alternative to intelligence as an attribute to God is to ascribe the nature of things to chance, it is hard to avoid the conclusion that some kind of planning is operative. If God acts *as if* God is intelligent, we can say that the model of mind or consciousness is applicable. The creative order of the universe is partially understood by human minds, and therefore the category of mind seems to be suitable. Furthermore, if we believe that some kind of interpersonal relationship with God is possible, this involves communication between minds. If God "knows" what is occurring, something akin to what we mean by consciousness is at work.

This leads into the question of whether we can think of God *as* personal, which is open to even more misrepresentation than other models. We may think of God talking to Moses in the burning bush, or of the "great Lord Jehovah" portrayed in a folk play with a "ten-cent *see*gar," or of the Sunday school vision of the old man with a beard sitting in his rocking chair listening to our prayers or to the broadcast of the Heavenly Choral and Harp Society. When we say that God may be thought of *as personal*, we do *not* mean that God is *a person*. The divine image of God may be impressed on the nature of human beings, but the human image must not be impressed upon God, even though the metaphor of the human person is helpful in thinking about God.

We may be helped by a linguistic distinction. The translation of the Lord's Prayer in the earlier versions (until 1881), began, "Our

Father, *which* art in heaven."[6] Grammatically, this use of *which* is a legal one referring to a *legal* rather than a human person. It is used in law for corporations as well as individuals to indicate the status of an entity in a law court. Therefore, we may say that when God is to be treated or thought of as a person, it is this legal usage that is meant.

When we say that God is personal, we mean that God has the *legal status* of a person in our thinking, that in some sense God is a spirit which is self-conscious and which responds to those who seek the Lord, absorbing our joys and sorrows and being affected by them, and providing the transforming and renewing powers which we experience through our relations with God. We are *not* saying that God is like a human person or a human mind, but that these analogies are all that we have to account for our experience of God as an actual entity which wills the good that is actually in the world and holds vast potentialities for the furthering of values in the world. God does this by participating in the processes of the cosmos, of history, of society, and of human lives.

No longer do we think of God as an irresponsible miracle-worker. Miracles reflect human ignorance rather than the glory of God. God is working through the whole of· reality in the face of stubborn resistance, and when we align ourselves with the aims of God our welfare is increased. We learn to read God's message in the laws of the universe and we come to an understanding of the miracle of God's reliability in a world in which chance and novelty are operating. What seem to be miracles of human transformation come when God's spirit enters our consciousness and we experience God's persuasive grace.

Unless we rely on sheer speculations unsupported by evidence, there is little that we can say about the origin of the cosmos and nothing about God as creator. God may well be the creator if the

---

6. *See The New Testament Octapla*, ed. Luther A. Weigle (New York: Thomas Nelson & Sons, n.d.), pp. 28–29. Also, the English *Book of Common Prayer* (1662). I am indebted to F. S. C. Northrop for this information.

universe had an origin in time, but the knowledge of God as being the creative order or force on which the cosmos depends is more important religiously than the belief that God is the creator. Whether there was ever an original creation is religiously unimportant, and the speculative answer to that question is the work of philosophers. The important fact for religious living is that *the creative process itself is a continuing one and is the working of God now*. If we are to live religiously and significantly, we must ally ourselves with the creative processes of God. If God works through the world as "the personality-evolving activities of the cosmos,"[7] then, in order to bring our own personalities to the fullness of their potentialities, we must fulfill the conditions of the spiritual and moral laws of personality development. God stands at the beginning of all religious commitment, and this faith is based on the insight that God is the one on whom all creation depends for its order, structure, and continuing existence.

We may believe that God is concerned with the ultimate happenings of life, although there may be limitations on the power to coerce. If there is genuine human freedom, God may be disobeyed; if there is genuine chance, the unpredictable may occur; if there is genuine novelty, even God may be surprised. If God is love, however, God fulfills the qualities required to meet most of our religious needs. It is doubtful, in the light of the evidence as we have portrayed it, that God predestines our activities or our salvation; but it is reasonable to hope that in the end God's aims will be fulfilled. God's power to draw things together, as the principle of integration, tends to win out over the forces of disintegration, and evil is always disintegrative and parasitic. God will cast out Satan.

If we think of God as having an initial aim or purpose for human beings, we are led to the consideration of God's functions in the light of human experience. The renewing and transforming power of God is at work in our midst, and this leads us more nearly to align our aims with God's initial aim. But God does more than this.

7. Shailer Mathews, *Growth of the Idea of God* (New York: Macmillan, 1931), p. 214.

From the beginning of the biblical story, God is represented as taking the initiative to bring people into line, to pay the price of salvation, to make people over. This comes to a dramatic high point in the story of the cross, when redemption is the theme of the death of Jesus as a way of leading people from their sins.

As people are reconciled with God, they are reconciled with each other. This seems to work both ways. We are told that we are enabled to love because God first loved us, and we cannot say that we love God unless we also love other human beings. We can show our love of God by showing it "to the least of these," and yet God's love for us is prior. Therefore, reconciliation is both a gift from God and a human act. God is redeemer and reconciler, and also the liberator who makes these things possible.

Thus, God is one who draws us into community. The organic nature of reality carries over into the social nature of humanity, so that the will to belong is primary in human aspirations. The concepts of the church as the people of God, of God as the giver of this sense of community, and of human beings as being drawn into fellowship as worshippers of God are essential to our understanding. God is present where human beings are together in God's name.

Furthermore, in our understanding of God at work, we discover God's ingression; God is immanent; God comes into human life. This leads to two fundamental religious principles: God's work is both incarnational and sacramental. There is a basis for our understanding of how God could be present in and work through Jesus as the Christ and of how God could be found in and through the sacraments of the church.

When we have said all these things about God, we still have not exhausted our insights into God's nature. We need to rely on a mixture of models, as well as on a series of names which can serve as models, such as Lord, King, High Tower, Shepherd, Light, Counselor, and Father. It is the use of Father which has been most widespread, especially in the address to God in prayer. It was a sure insight when Jesus called God "Father." Perhaps he was profoundly influenced by Joseph. Although we suspect that Jesus' father died while Jesus was still young, it is probable that Joseph left an indelible impression which grew with the years in spite of the opposition of the rest of the family to his mission. When Jesus turned to his contemporary Jewish tradition for an analogy for speaking of his relationship with God, no other word but *Father* would do. Jesus said, "Show yourselves true sons of your Father in heaven, for he makes his sun to rise on good and bad alike, and makes the rain fall on the upright and wrongdoers" (Mt. 5:45–46,G). "I tell you," said Jesus, "love your enemies and pray for your persecutors, so that you may show yourselves true sons of your Father in heaven" (Mt. 5:44–45a). Jesus was selective about the attributes of fatherhood that he applied to God. It was the projection of an ideal, not the divinization of human fatherhood. Certain elements of fatherhood are rejected in this model, for example, a father's finiteness, partiality, maleness, sexuality, and (at least for Jesus) absolute power. Furthermore, some of the attributes applied to God as Father seem to be feminine. At least, then, as Ian T. Ramsey suggests, the model of divine Father is "a little problematical," and we must decide *"which* developmental inferences are *reliable."*[8] The model probably cannot stand alone even when properly qualified, and we should mix it in with other models.

## A Dipolar God

When we think of God in terms of process philosophy, we have to understand the way in which the process is structured. We can imagine abstract forms, or potentialities waiting to be born, or even a primordial reality that structures what would otherwise be chaos. Without some kind of direction, limitation, or persuasion, life would be like a river that has no banks, a flood with no dike to

8. *Models and Mystery* (New York: Oxford University Press, 1964), pp. 59–60.

control it. With no aims or goals in mind, life would go on in a chaotic sort of way, if at all, but there would be no goal.

If we think of God as a creative order, we are joining together two basic ideas: the ordering and the creating aspects of God. When Whitehead spoke of the "primordial" nature or aspect of God, he had in mind the abstract element, as the subjective aims of God work through eternal forms. When he spoke of the consequent nature or aspects of God, he was thinking of the immanent process which is at work in our midst, which we experience, and which is the persuasive love of the Galilean vision. It is God's grace, God's free gift of self, God's consequent nature.

Other writers have made similar distinctions. We can think of God as abstract perfection and as concrete manifestation. Thus we can say that God's abstract nature is everlasting and cannot change, while God's concrete nature is participating in the life of the universe and is affected by events as they occur. God can suffer, enjoy, and change. So God affects history and changes and adapts with historical events. God participates in the process of becoming, operating chiefly through persuasion and only becoming rigid when the structures are abused. Insofar as we share in the subjective aims of God, we are on the right track. But these changes in God are not imperfections; for God remains unsurpassable except by self.

This involvement of God with the world and the world with God leads some theologians to speak of *panentheism.* God is not the all, as in pantheism, and God is not separated from the world, as in deism. God is both cause and effect; God is independent as primordial and involved as consequent; God is good and yet knows and suffers from evil. Using the human organism as a model, we can say that all things are in God and yet there is an independent identity that marks God off from the universe. It is like our self-identity in the midst of change.

It is through union with God "that we live and move and exist" (Acts 17:28,G). In God we "come to life, . . . are motivated, . . . find meaning" (CP). This dipolar deity, one God in which the abstract is included within the concrete, is the source of our life and its meaning and therefore of our power for goodness. We experience a power which does for us what we otherwise cannot do. This power is found wherever and whenever we are aware of certain kinds of tenderness and love in human relations, and it is at work throughout the universe. This is what we mean by grace, the free gift of God's love, given to us in our predicaments. It helps us overcome our alienation from other human beings, from the animal world, and from nature. It makes possible a reverence for the natural world in which we all participate, as well as awe before God who is the source of our becoming and perishing.

## Evil

We have insisted that we interpret God's nature in terms of love and persuasion, so that God's goodness may be unlimited but not all-powerful. When we take seriously the model of Father as an approach to God's nature, we have to allow for the behavior of children. If we take into consideration the presence of chance and the unpredictability of an open future, we can account for much that is evil. Evil is thought of as a brute motive force, but an unstable one that tends toward disintegration, something like a cancer. Whitehead wrote that "the fact of the instability of evil is the moral order of the world."[9] The moral forces, including God and humanity, are tested by the presence of evil. God knows that there is evil, and as God prehends the evil and takes it into consciousness it can be transformed, but our command to "overcome evil with good" (Rom. 12:21, RSV) stands as a challenge as we ally ourselves with what we conceive to be God's purpose.

Violence, especially as it leads to suffering and death, is an obvious evil, particularly in warfare. There was a time when gods were associated with war and victory, and an imperialist civil

9. Alfred N. Whitehead, *Religion in the Making* (New York: Macmillan, 1926), p. 95.

religion still has war gods. But we run into difficulties when we try to associate a God of love with any violence that denies the value of human beings. Does God want war? Could God stop war?

The relation between God and human beings is such that we have freedom to do many things contrary to the will of God. We talk about God's love, and then proceed to deny that love in our relations with other persons, in our attention to the laws of health or economics, and in political and military relations. When we consistently ignore God's laws and expectations, in time there will come eras of darkness and even the ends of civilizations. We are at the end of an era because we are reaping that which we have sown. We have sown seeds of hate and distrust, of greed and selfishness, of imperialism and nationalism, and now the first fruits—or perhaps the last fruits—are at hand.

Does God, then, cause war? Yes—and no! The laws of God are such that war, suffering, and the end of an era are brought about by acts of free human beings, although it often seems as if we are caught up in a compulsion to wage war. The tragedy of God's judgment is that it is applied impersonally and impartially. Vile living causes the inheritance of social disease. The innocent lose their rights along with those who deserve punishment. War is wholesale, brutal murder—mostly of the innocent. However, it is clear that we all share in the guilt of war.

There is another side to the question. *God does not want war!* God wants the kingdom to come on earth, a kingdom of peace to those of goodwill. God sees the sins of humanity being carried to neighbors and future generations. We may believe that God's loving response to this is to share in the human suffering. God suffers with both sides in all wars. This insight into God's nature does not alter our responsibility to make decisions on complex grounds when faced with the question of war, but any decision to wage war must be the lesser of two evils.

Social evils can be explained by the activity of free human beings and the structure of society we have developed. There are many situations in the field of social relations which are opposed to God's aim for humankind. God's fundamental nature as creative agent leads to activities seeking to influence entities or persons who choose to offer resistance. God is limited by the logical structure of reality. God does not will what is evil, and therefore whatever is evil is opposed to God. But we are free to create evil because we can oppose God's will. Evil is something just as real as goodness; it possesses an actual malignancy that can take possession of us.

Christian theology has not yet come to terms with the holocaust. The deaths of six million Jews destroyed belief in God for many people. We cannot write off such an evil, any more than we can ignore deaths on slave ships, the slaughter of native Americans, or wanton destruction in wars. The evil is of such magnitude that a God who willed it would be unworthy of worship.

Many attempts have been made to explain God's relation to evil and suffering. If God is in complete control and is unchanging in every aspect, so that he is impassible and immutable, then all we can do (logically) is throw up our hands, although (psychologically) we never do this even when the situation seems hopeless. So our response to evil includes a denial of the traditional teaching that God determines what will happen and has the power to overrule what is going on. William James was so sensitive to this problem that he postulated a pluralistic universe in which God is one process among many, for God has an environment and there is opposition against which to struggle. Edgar S. Brightman thought that within God's nature there is a "given" which leads to evil and cannot be controlled completely. Robert L. Calhoun preferred to think of God's limitations as both within and without, for God is faced by "rigidities" in the structure of the world which, while not bad in themselves, contribute to the hampering of God's work in concrete situations.

A God of persuasive love is not powerless. Even the model of love as applied to God needs to be modified by other models, including those of justice and goodness, and therefore judgment is always possible. It may be that God has all the power there is, which is different from being all-powerful, because there are other powers at work in the universe. Unexpected evil as well as unpredictable good may come out of the chance meeting of two activities or entities. The principle of indeterminism points to chance at the center of the activities of electrons. The ways in which processes come together may result in something novel. Thus we have earthquakes and hurricanes, accidents and sickness, changes in the weather, and catastrophes, which lead to suffering and are seen by us as evil. In such situations, the psalmist is on the right track when he writes, "God is our refuge and strength, a very present help in trouble" (Ps. 46:1,RSV).

William James gave us an interesting analogy. If we conceive of life as a gigantic chess game, with God as the master player and ourselves as novices, God controls the game but not the individual moves of the players. There is real chance, real freedom, and God leaves the decisions and moves up to us. There are real possibilities and responsibilities facing us, and we need to work at the problems. In some cases, God helps us to solve them, but often we do it ourselves. In this world of chance, novelty, freedom, evil, and goodness, we may be certain that the world is safe, and God knows "that no matter how much it might zig-zag, he could surely bring it home at last."[10]

## THE CHRISTIAN GOD

The essential teachings of Jesus and the historic Christian teachings about the nature of God are acceptable to today's world when presented in terms such as these. God can be observed at work in the world, or at least after reflection on our experiences we interpret events as due to God's activity. Those of insight and genius see more deeply into God's nature, and when these ways of thinking are brought to light, the rest of us can say, "Yes, God was

10. See William James, "The Dilemma of Determinism," in *The Will to Believe and Other Essays in Popular Philosophy* (New York: Longmans, Green & Co., 1896), pp. 180–183.

there all the time, only we did not see this." Jesus could see God at work in the lilies of the field, and he taught that not even a sparrow could fall to the ground without God's knowing it. We, too, can see that now. Jesus taught that God is like a Father and our relation to God is that of children; but also that we are responsible for carrying out our own activities. We can understand this, too. Jesus taught that the love, mercy, and judgment of God were at work in our lives, and throughout history these attributes have been validated in the experiences of average men and women. Never should our devotion be to a God we do not know, or to the word or symbol which stands for God. Never should faith be based on guesswork. There is much about God that is mysterious, and God's ways are higher than our ways  but *the God we know is with us,* and our destiny depends upon the completeness of our commitment to the reality, the process, the actual entity for which the word *God* stand ⸺

# 5
# *Who Was Jesus?*

The most fascinating and perplexing of all people is Jesus of Nazareth. Many people feel that they know him better than anyone who has ever lived, and yet we know so little about him that his biography would fill but a few pages. The ways and means of seeking to know the details of Jesus' life have been many and varied. Scholars have not agreed in their evaluation of the data, in their interpretation of the significance of the events recorded, or in the normal prejudices with which everyone must face this problem. Although the sources cannot be handled without bias, we must deal as impartially as we can with the evidence. The method of the modern historical school is a naturalistic one, and every attempt must be made to explore and explain the facts according to the same norms as we would use to recapture the life of an Egyptian pharaoh or George Washington.

We must rely to a great extent on the most competent scholars in the field, so that we will have the advantage of the best tools with which to work. The lives of Jesus of popular literature, of church school lessons, and of an older generation fail to present either accuracy or sound history. Recent scholars have warned us against mistaken approaches, and many intelligent Christians are skeptical of what they have been taught. The life of Jesus has received the most rigorous study of any life in history, and even so there is a paucity of fact. In order to obtain a consistent picture, free from theological prejudices and presuppositions, we first must rely on those scholars who deal most impartially and appreciatively with the available data, and then read the synoptic Gospels for ourselves.

## THE SOURCES

The non-Christian sources have little value. At their best, all they do is corroborate the fact of the historical existence of Jesus, without providing any details. The accounts of Jesus in the non-canonical Gospels provide some fascinating accounts that rarely if ever seem to be based on what actually happened. The Dead Sea Scrolls add to our background knowledge of Jesus' times, but so far there is no evidence of any connection between Jesus and his followers and the Qumran community. A careful and critical use of the first three Gospels, especially the essence of Mark and the sayings known as "Q" in Matthew and Luke, provides the primary data. The rest of the New Testament, especially Acts and the letters of Paul, is instructive, as it indicates the impact of Jesus upon his followers and the evolution of the church from the messianic hopes of the disciples.

The real difficulty, however, is not in the paucity of evidence but in the preconceived ideas, the theological biases, and the modern-mindedness of contemporary scholarship. We must beware of "the peril of modernizing Jesus," which began when the first words were written about him, as Henry J. Cadbury reminded us.[1] Even the synoptic Gospels were written from the point of view of the primitive church, and there are several layers of tradition that we need to work back through, a process that is difficult and risky. The Gospels are not primarily history; they are interpretations aimed to convert readers to the "good news" of Christian faith. They see Jesus through the eyes of the church, in the light of theological development, and through the dynamic resurrection experiences of the early apostles. The outlook of the first-century

---

1. Cf. Henry J. Cadbury, *The Peril of Modernizing Jesus* (New York: Macmillan, 1937), p. 17.

Jewish mind had not yet been lost, but they express a point of view quite removed from that of Jesus of Nazareth. They present a messianic interpretation, which does not quite eliminate a more primitive view. There is a foretelling of Jesus' death and resurrection on the basis of Old Testament prophecy and Jesus' assumed self-consciousness, which is a natural addition *after* the event. The church is taken for granted, although Jesus expected the coming of the kingdom of God. There is a confusion of the theory of the early church's views with those of Jesus concerning the end of the age (eschatology). These considerations make accurate use of the sources difficult.

With our increased knowledge of the backgrounds of Jesus' ministry, our insight into the first-century Jewish mind, especially with the new knowledge from the Dead Sea Scrolls, and our ability to distinguish the various strata in the development of tradition, we have some tools which help in clarifying the mist which has hidden Jesus through many centuries. Even with these aids, the findings are sparse and tentative and scholars still express wide disagreement. The following statements, therefore, are not final in any sense, but they do represent the common opinions of a selected group of scholars who, in the opinion of this writer, have a right to be followed in our thinking.

## The Life of Jesus

*Backgrounds.* We do know something of Jesus' religious environment. He inherited the great tradition of the Jewish religion. This meant knowledge of the greatness, glory, and goodness of Yahweh, of whom the Jews were the chosen people, in a covenant relationship. Tied in with this was the expectation of the end of the age, when a messiah would appear. This hope turned in two directions: (1) the arrival of a political messiah, whom Yahweh would aid in overcoming the enemy, and (2) the intervention of Yahweh by means of a supernatural messiah. These two schools of thought ranged side by side. The latter was further developed by the influence of Persian dualism. Another variant depended on whether the kingdom would come on earth or in heaven. Furthermore, Jesus inherited the practices of the synagogue, the duties of the law, and the ethical demands of prophetic religion. Add to this great heritage the ability of a sensitive spirit to delve more deeply into reality than others, and we have the major elements in the background of Jesus' teaching and mission.

*His Ministry.* It is generally agreed that we know nothing of Jesus until his appearance at the time of his baptism. It is most likely that he was born in Nazareth in 4–6 B.C., the first-born of simple Galilean parents. Except for the nativity narratives, there are no references to Jesus' connection with Bethlehem, and he was always thought of as from Nazareth or Galilee. There were at least six other children, and we know the names of his four brothers. His family was opposed to his ministry (Mark 3:21–35, 6:1–6; Mt. 13:53–58; Lk. 4:16–30).

The earliest sources (Mark, the early Gospel source called Q, the letters of Paul, and perhaps the first version of Luke) indicate no evidence of a miraculous birth, or even of the appearance in the temple of the young boy. The Christmas stories have great value as attempts to explain the significance of the man sent from God. They are legends which contain a fundamental truth about the nature of Jesus. Their importance as religious myth cannot be overestimated, and they have a permanent place in Christian literature, but they are not history and are not necessary for the doctrine of the incarnation. Even Bishop Charles Gore, who believed in the virgin birth, did not think it was part of the original apostolic message.[2] Throughout the Gospels, it is assumed that Joseph was the father of the Nazarene. James, the brother of Jesus, became the head of the Jerusalem church as a right of inheritance as

2. Charles Gore, *A New Commentary on Holy Scripture* (New York: Macmillan, 1928), p. 315.

well as a "witness to the resurrection." In the early church, we may conclude, there was no great concern about the birth of Jesus.

It is probable that Jesus' ministry was inspired by the teachings and fate of John the Baptist, but whatever other causes there may have been are obscured by the tradition. Jesus' original message was most likely a repetition of John's preaching to repent, for the end of the age was coming. From the time of its inception, the events of Jesus' ministry occurred one after the other during only a short period. Few scholars today accept the chronology in John, and many do not accept the order in Mark. The events recorded in Mark could have happened within a period of from six months to a year. We may estimate that Jesus began his ministry in 28 A.D. and that he was crucified in the spring of 29. During this brief time, he gathered about him a devoted band of men and women, and wandered all over Galilee, teaching and preaching and performing some acts of healing. It is hard to determine how successful he was. The hope of the people for some type of messiah may have drawn many to him, and certainly his teachings appealed to others. It is probable, however, that he never had a large following, and the number of his listeners has been magnified by the tradition. Even in the Palm Sunday story, the fact that people hailed him would not necessarily indicate that they were his followers.

The facts of Jesus' life fit into this skeleton outline. We know a few more things that are significant. There were the appeal of his teachings, the gathering of loyal women and men about him, the mounting hostility of the ecclesiastical and political powers, and finally his death. In between these facts, we discover something of his purpose, his teachings, and his person, all of which give us historical data for the beginnings of a Christology. Ultimately, the resurrection appearances, however they are interpreted, provide the basis for faith in Jesus as Lord.

*His Purpose.* If Jesus' career moved with the swiftness indicated by the brevity of his teaching ministry, he must have been

motivated by a main purpose. The central theme was the an-
nouncement of the imminent coming of the kingdom of God. It is
entirely possible that when Jesus took his disciples to Jerusalem, he
expected the coming of the kingdom to be consummated at that
very Passover. He did not go there because he expected to be put to
death or because he foresaw his resurrection, but because his burning hope was to be realized. The early form of Luke supports this
thesis:

> When the time came, he took his place at the table, with
> the apostles about him. And he said to them,
>    "I have greatly desired to eat this Passover with you
> [before I suffer]. For I tell you, I will never eat one
> again until it reaches its fulfillment in the kingdom of God."
>    And when he was handed a cup, he thanked God, and then
> said.
>    "Take this and share it among you, for I tell you, I
> will not drink the product of the vine again until the kingdom
> of God comes" (Lk. 22:14–18, G).

It is hard to read this impartially without concluding that Jesus
was not expecting a long period of abstinence but that he expected
some quick action on God's part. Whether this coming kingdom
would be a social revolution or a supernatural transformation of all
that is cannot be decided, but that he expected God to act seems
clear from this reading.

There is doubt among some scholars as to whether Jesus ever
considered himself to be the messiah. As we know, *messiah* applied
to two points of view, political and eschatological. Jesus explicitly
rejected the former, and his references to the latter, in spite of
careful editing, seem to refer to another. After the resurrection, it
was natural enough for the apostles to conclude that Jesus was the
messiah, but the concept was not of a Jewish messiah, however, for
the term had been radicalized in the light of the resurrection. When
Jesus was crucified, the label pinned on him was "King of the Jews."

From this fact, we can draw no conclusions about his own self-consciousness, but the chances are that he did not think of himself as the messiah.[3] As Enslin wrote, "It is one thing for a first-century Jew to have expected a figure soon to appear; a totally different thing for him to believe that he himself would be miraculously transformed from a flesh-and-blood man into this figure. With all allowances made, it is hard to conceive how such a view could have been held except at the expense of moral sanity."[4]

If Jesus never claimed to be a political or eschatological messiah, there are still two alternatives: (1) he may have established himself as the suffering servant, drawing upon Isaiah, or (2) he may have been considered simply as a prophet. It seems likely that the concept of Jesus as suffering servant arose to explain the crucifixion, which Jesus did not anticipate at least until the very last moment, and which was an embarrassment to the disciples whenever they made claims for their new sect. It was an interpretation naturally read back into the record after the resurrection and long before there were any written reports.

Some want to use the term *rabbi*, but Jews did not use this title until after Jesus' time. Certainly the priest concept in Hebrews is late. Perhaps it is best to claim simply that in some sense Jesus was in the prophetic tradition, as a Jewish lay person with a special commission. The problem cannot easily be solved. The solution which seems to me to offer the least difficulty, on the basis of the synoptic evidence when stripped of its postresurrection accretions, is that Jesus believed he was called by God to a particular mission: *the pronouncement of the imminence of God's kingdom and the means for entering therein.* The center of Jesus' religion was never himself; the heart of his message was the call of God's kingdom, and God was the center of all his teachings and living. His mission was messianic, and after the resurrection the disciples came to the conclusion that he was the messiah, although this was never clearly

3. See Nils Alstrup Dahl, *The Crucified Messiah* (Minneapolis: Augsburg, 1975), pp. 23–36.
4. Morton S. Enslin, *Christian Beginnings* (New York: Harper & Row, 1939), p. 163.

defined. Many attributes were assigned to him, and as time went on there were many models by which he could be described, but none of them seemed to exhaust his meaning. The verdict of the disciples and the decision of history are written in the record of Christianity, that surely here was a man like no other, and he is deserving of our adulation and discipleship.

*His Teachings.* The teachings of Jesus can be best understood in the light of his Jewish heritage. He thought of himself as within the Jewish community and faith. Most of his teachings were drawn from this tradition, and many Christian apologists make too sweeping claims for Jesus' originality. The originality of Jesus lay in his selection of materials for his purpose rather than in the creation of new ideas. He thought of his teachings as the fulfillment of the law, even though he saw clearly that the laws were made for humanity and not the reverse, and therefore he got into trouble with his liberal interpretation, for example, of laws about the Sabbath. Jesus had the type of mind which brings into a single focus many varying ideas from different sources, and his synthesizing power was such that the result seemed to be a new creation, which had the undeniable stamp of his personality. The two great commandments, to love God and one's neighbor, were brought together by Jesus from two different books, and they were equated in such a way that they cannot again be divided, but is is likely that other Jewish sages did the same thing.

We cannot escape the *eschatological framework* of his teachings. Jesus really believed that the kingdom was soon to appear through a catastrophic act on God's part. So one must repent and be ready for the act of God which was to come. This was Jesus' earliest and constant message. Except by misreading the synoptic Gospels through the eyes of the Fourth Gospel, it is impossible to establish any "spiritual" kingdom. The kingdom of God means more than this, but it always implied the sovereignty of God in this world.

Jesus' *call to repentance* is based upon this conviction concerning the kingdom. The precondition to entrance into the kingdom is repentance, for God is not only the sovereign master and judge, but also is full of love and tenderness. Jesus was typically prophetic in making the prerequisite to membership in the kingdom a moral one. He talked about the lost sheep of Israel, but there is nothing in his teaching which specifically rejects the Gentiles. His moral demand outranked the legal requirements of the law and superceded the nationalistic emphasis of the contemporary Judaism of that time.

Although Jesus remained within his tradition even in his *ethical emphasis*, it is this which was distinctive. The implications of his ethics could not be held within national bounds, and they have taken on a universal form of appeal which has been self-validating through the ages. Furthermore, the ethical quality of repentance purifies the concept of God. The moral and spiritual relationship which, Jesus taught, can exist between an individual and God takes precedence over the demands of the immediate environment. When we repent and come to ourselves, we turn to God and God receives us. This is the means to entering the kingdom, and the parable of the Prodigal Son stands as a beacon of hope for all of us who truly seek God, and it stands as a warning to those who would make salvation a legal scheme.

In Jesus' ethical statements, it is his *view of human beings* which stands out. He had a higher regard for persons and their potentialities than many of his immediate and later followers. He was painfully aware of the sinful aspects of human nature, but he never taught that people are inherently sinful. He saw the same potential for *becoming* children of God in the Pharisee and the Publican. The tragedy of sin is that it frustrates the emergence of moral and spiritual growth and alienates us from God. Without dimming his eyes to sin, Jesus held out the hope of salvation for us all.

The constant factor in Jesus' ethics lies in his emphasis on our intention or attitude. Once our attitude is right, we can be counted on to make external conditions correct. There is a relativity about the values to be sought, and the ends attained may not be of equal worth, but we are judged by our intentions. This does not eliminate the importance of consequences, but emphasizes the organic relation between the intention and the result, between the tree and the fruit it bears.

Salvation, then, does not depend on any special transaction, but on what one does about one's own sins. The idea of a sacrificial redemption developed later as an explanation of the crucifixion, and it superceded the highly moral and spiritual insight of Jesus. Yet salvation does not depend on how good we are, for that becomes moralism rather than morality and leads to self-righteousness. It is a matter of relationships between ourselves and God as well as with other persons, and this is measured in terms of love as well as justice.

Jesus selected the highest and best from his ethical environment. Although no such discourse as the Sermon on the Mount was ever delivered as such, it is probable that except for the literary form and certain embellishments, it is representative of the religious ethics of Jesus in both forms, in Matthew and Luke. What we find here are moral *attitudes* rather than principles or norms, although these latter are implied. These attitudes express the central aspects of Jesus' religion, and they have proved themselves sound no matter how in error Jesus may have been concerning the time of the coming kingdom.

The *motives* behind these teachings concerning attitudes are not simply those of altruism. Jesus appealed to the motives of fear and reward. In the Beatitudes, the poor, the meek, the peacemakers, and others are happy because of what is going to happen to them. They obviously are not happy now in their poverty and suffering. When the kingdom comes, they will be liberated and free to be their best selves, and thus distinctions between wealth and privilege on the one hand and poverty and submission on the other will vanish. This is not the message of self-centered individualism, for the goal of such religious faith is primarily social and God-centered. The earthly kingdom is a constant challenge, and the rewards are sufficiently tangible to provide the stimulus for Christian living.

When we talk of Jesus' *religious teachings*, we find ourselves in the midst of the greatest difficulties. The sources are overladen with tradition at this point, and there is always the unconscious desire to preserve our own private interests. We need to remind ourselves that Jesus was a Jew and not a Christian; he was consciously Jewish from beginning to end. The Gospels were written later from the point of view of a small group which had been expelled from the Jewish community as a radical sect. If we recall, also, that we can expect no theological *system* to emerge from the thought of Jesus, this will keep us from interpreting his statements from the standpoint of the demands of modern logic. Jesus' teachings centered in the kingdom, and the kingdom was for him essentially a religious concept. The means for entrance into this kingdom lay primarily in moral and spiritual attitudes, both of which were conceived religiously and as part of the Hebraic tradition.

Jesus' idea of God was consistent with his inheritance. Yahweh's attitudes are the same: absolute master, judge, holy, righteous. God is near to us, and there is a greater emphasis on the love and mercy of God. Jesus believed in a personal God, who is at work in the cosmos and in nature. Jesus took nature more seriously than traditional Christianity has, even to seeing God's concern for the lilies in the field and the birds. With this concept of God, religious living is firmly grounded in the realities of everyday experience. God is near, the kingdom is at hand, and if we turn to God we shall be saved. God is a present help, a loving companion, and the judge of humanity in history and in nature. We have freedom either to obey or to disobey God, and we can make this choice and take the consequences.

Jesus never put the emphasis on himself. His religion was centered in God. He believed that he was called to a unique mission, as a messenger of God, and he carried this out until finally it led to his death as a criminal. He was concerned with human beings and their welfare, and he preached to them in terms of the amazing implications of what the sovereignty of God could mean for their lives. And so he was crucified.

*Trial, Death, and Resurrection.* Historic Christianity has always put particular credence in the story of Holy Week because the events are recounted by all four evangelists. Some believe that it is an accurate historical record, except perhaps for some details. Others think that the completeness of the story indicates that the accounts reflect a later form, and that a thorough investigation of the sources causes a collapse of practically the whole structure. Certainly there is some historical material in the drama of Holy Week. We can see how it became necessary to get rid of this preacher who stirred up the people and filled them with hopes about overcoming oppression. Jesus was not defended against what was probably trumped-up evidence.

It is hard to get at the facts of the trial, for the story has a good deal of symbolic material. Some scholars doubt that the claim that Jesus was the messiah would have led to his death at the hands of the Romans, but that as an agitator or false prophet this was a possibility. The inscription, "King of the Jews," occurs with such definiteness that it may be factual. If so, the crucified messiah concept, which is central to Christian faith, must be postponed until after the resurrection.[5] Jesus, from the point of view of the Gospel writers, was obviously innocent. It is not clear who interrogated Jesus or what the final charges were. Gerard S. Sloyan summarizes his study as follows: "The man Jesus was dispatched in quite unusual circumstances in an age given to violence. We should not shrink from the harsh realities that attended this particular reality. What exactly they were is hard to discover. Only a small portion of the data is recoverable. When recovered it will not redound to the credit of the band of threatened men of both nations, Israel and Rome, who saw to his judicial murder."[6]

The stories of the events after the crucifixion are inconsistent. They narrate different incidents and give divergent interpretations. All four Gospels are needed, for example, to obtain the so-called seven last words of Jesus. Mark cuts his story at 16:8, leaving us to conjecture whether there was an original ending beyond this point

5. See Dahl, *Crucified Messiah*, pp. 23–24.
6. Gerard S. Sloyan, *Jesus on Trial* (Philadelphia: Fortress, 1973), p. 134.

and whether it was destroyed because. it contradicted a more popular account.

Nils A. Dahl writes that "in contrast to the life and death of Jesus his resurrection cannot be made an object of historical research. Only the Easter faith of the disciples is accessible to the historian, the origin of which he can illuminate only to a certain degree."[7] A likely conjecture is that there was a primary experience, either of the women or of Peter, followed by some group experiences. From these experiences the stories arose as attempts to account for the facts, and probably assumed their present form about 70 A.D. *The important thing for us to observe is the result of the resurrection in the lives of the women and the disciples.* This is the empirical fact, open to historical reconstruction: Jesus' followers were changed from defeated cowards into persons who were instrumental in converting the known world to their new religion. Every extreme from the physical raising of Jesus' body to some type of hallucination has been used to explain the event, but the explanation is secondary, and the fact of transformed persons is primary. It is from this perspective that the life of Jesus takes on a deeper meaning.

The resurrection is the most vital point in the development of Christianity. No matter how it happened or what happened, the results determined the future of Western religion. The resurrection experience not only galvanized the disciples into action, it also convinced them that Jesus was the messiah promised in the Jewish tradition, although the concept was radicalized, and this combination set forth forces that led to the development of the church, which Jesus did not foresee at any time in his ministry. The church makes it possible for us to conceive of Jesus alive in and through human beings today, and provides a pathway whereby we may come into the presence of God. Because of this present-day experience, Easter is as meaningful today as it was twenty centuries ago.

7. Dahl, *Crucified Messiah*, p. 76.

## The Historical Jesus

We have four portraits of Jesus. These portraits give us insights into his nature, even when what is recorded arises from faith and legend, for these stories, too, are part of the historical record of Jesus' impact on the early Christian community. Something compelling in these stories makes us say that "his moral grandeur, his beautiful spirituality, his dauntless courage, his forward moving step, his sure apprehension of life, all are unmistakably signs of his leadership."[8]

The Jesus revealed by critical study of the Gospels is the Jesus of the Christian faith, and our thoughts of the incarnation must be wrapped up intimately with our evaluation of Jesus and our acceptance of his concept of God. God, somehow, was in Jesus, and we must try to understand how this could be so. But we must not use our faith in Christ to supplement our inadequate historical knowledge of the man Jesus, for that is to borrow illegitimately. However, the historical evidence does not stop here. The Christian Church did evolve, and it claimed that Jesus was the messiah. To some extent this claim was based on what the church remembered about the actual Jesus of Nazareth, but it also had another foundation in the resurrection and Pentecost accounts, and in the development of beliefs based on the corporate experience of the community. To this problem we now turn.

8. Ray O. Miller, *Modernist Studies in the Life of Jesus* (Boston: Sherman, French, 1917), p. 51.

# 6
# *What about Christ?*

The Jesus who actually lived is the same Jesus who was experienced as alive after he had died and is the risen Christ of Christians today. It is important to see these connections, and to place them in proper perspective. We shall see that if God is immanent, is incarnational, is ingredient in our lives, and if God incorporates our suffering and our joys, we can make the necessary connection between Jesus of Nazareth and the Christ of faith.

There are two common approaches to the study of the nature of Christ. The traditional way has been to start with his divinity, saying that Jesus is in some way God, and then to account for his limitations. Usually this has divorced Christology from the historic Jesus, and the emphasis has been on an impersonal theory of Jesus' humanity. The other approach has been to begin with the historic Jesus, tracing out the developments of interpretations of his nature, until finally the attributes of divinity are applied to him.

The obvious place to begin, in today's world, is with the historical evidence. As F. R. Barry has reminded us, "Because we begin to know how things are done, we cannot simply assume that God doesn't do them."[1] Just because we can trace the natural origins of Jesus and the church, we do not need to exclude a theological interpretation of what happened. We may assume that the cogency of our argument concerning the nature of Christ depends on the accuracy and persuasiveness of the historical and experimental evidence.

---

1. *Christianity and Psychology* (New York: Doran, n.d.), p. 172.

Historical study of the Gospels gives us first of all a bare skeleton. Jesus was a typical, but superior, Jewish prophet, who conceived himself as within the prophetic tradition with a unique message. He was surrounded by a small band of men and women, and went his way, teaching and doing good. The essence of his teaching was repentance in the light of the coming of the kingdom, and this repentance involved moral and spiritual change. In his own life he was in a close and even intimate relation with God, especially in his practice of prayer. There was a consistency between his teaching and his conduct that became the center of his proclamation. In his conduct he showed a certain disregard for some of the laws, and this led to severe criticism. He was considered a threat to both religious and political forces. Finally, he met with the opposition of the Roman and Jewish authorities and was crucified. As a result of later experiences, the little band was energized and enlarged, and in time an organization developed which was forced to break away from the synagogues. The center of this movement was the recollected person of Jesus, conceived of as the Messiah who would come again soon. The early Christians lived in expectation of the great consummation. Only as the generation of disciples died did there come to be any writing about Jesus, and the Gospels were written in the light of these later experiences to lead others to believe in the Christ.

The story is not told thus baldly, and the significance of these events is not immediately apparent without the myths, legends, and other forms of interpretation which are present throughout the New Testament. There was a development of Christology from the time of the resurrection on, and Christians are still wrestling with this problem.

The clearest statement of Christology in the New Testament was made by Paul in his letter to the Philippians: "Though he possessed the nature of God, he did not grasp at equality with God, but laid it aside to take on the nature of a slave and become like other men. When he had assumed human form, he still further humbled himself and carried his obedience so far as to die, and to die upon a cross. That is why God has so greatly exalted him, and given him the name above all others, so that in the name of Jesus every one should kneel, in heaven and on earth and in the underworld, and every one should acknowledge Jesus Christ as Lord, and thus glorify God the Father" (Phil. 2:6–11,G). Paul said that first of all the Son of God gave up all attributes of deity when he became a man, and because as a man he was fully obedient to the Father, *therefore* he has been exalted. Paul gloried in Jesus' humanity, and in it he saw God's movement of redemption for all who have faith. There is a paradox here, and we cannot press these statements too far.

In the Fourth Gospel this paradox was not kept, and the Logos who became flesh never ceased to be God. This distorts the meaning of the incarnation as given by Paul, because, for Paul, only as we give ourselves in complete submission to God *and* God gives grace to us can there be redemption. When the freedom of Jesus to respond as a human being to God is lost, the Logos becomes an automaton.

The early church even went further than this, and gave the doctrine of the nature of Christ precise formulation at the Council of Chalcedon. This formula acknowledged Christ to exist "in two natures unconfusedly, unchangeably, indivisibly, inseparably." He is "coessential with the Father as regards his deity, and the same coessential with us as regards his humanity." The formula is intricate, it is based on a world view and an anthropology that are no longer appropriate, but it strikes the pattern of a continuing orthodoxy. What it does is to deny the real humanity of Jesus, for it implies that Jesus' humanity was impersonal. Certainly, in the light of current process thought, we can do better than this.

Some will argue that Jesus claimed to be God in his earthly life, but this is an obvious and definite historical error. It is doubtful if he claimed to be the messiah, much less to be God. Furthermore, how could any such being as described in the Council of Chalcedon have had any personal religion of his own, as described in the synoptic Gospels? Jesus could have felt united with God in moments of religious experience, which is a common report of many religious persons, but he also understood himself to be under orders as a servant of God as well as a servant of others.

## THE BASIS OF CHRISTOLOGY

If we believe that God works by communicating love through persons, we may assume that the picture of Jesus portrayed in the Gospels is an adequate basis for Christology. First of all, Jesus was wholly human, exemplifying the best that we can conceive. This is evident in the records of his activities: his sympathetic healing, his kindness, his courage, his righteous indignation concerning the evils of his day, his fellowship with the poor and downtrodden, and his teaching. Second, he could see possibilities in other people. He picked his disciples from among the common people (of which he was one), and only one of them failed him in the end. The others were not consistently loyal, but before the story concludes they became the leaders of a great new movement. The potentialities were there, and Jesus saw them. The despised tax collector, the harlot, the outcast who confessed his sins, the Samaritan, and all who were considered unclean by the official priesthood found a response in Jesus to the goodness that resided in them. He treated women with a new kind of respect as human beings, and women responded by being among his followers. Third, Jesus had insight into the social and political problems that faced him and his generation. He rejected material revolution and put his faith in a spiritual revolution, although this often stirs people to revolt. There is no five-year plan for salvation in the Gospels, but the principles underlying every form of human liberation are found there. Fourth, Jesus saw more clearly into the nature of God than others. This is paramount in his message, and all that he was, said, or did is derived from the fundamental relationship between Jesus and God. Jesus' mission and message were essentially religious, and, for him, the basis for all human activity rested in the relationship between God and human beings. Fifth, this came to a head in the fact that he suffered. Suffering means to take upon one's self the feelings, joys, sorrows, and pains of others; to act and be acted upon; to endure and to respond. The life of Jesus included this kind of suffering, and we find it in sharp focus in the story of the cross.[2]

We intuitively sense a numinous quality in Jesus. The picture of Jesus with a light or halo shining about his head is not absurd, because it points to our response to him. We cannot read the Gospels without responding with an attitude of respect, reverence, and even awe. There is a uniqueness about Jesus' humanity which marks him off from other persons. In the words of R. D. Richardson, he is different from others, "different as diamonds are from charcoal though both be composed of the same stuff—because the divine image in which God created [us] is seen in him alone in its full glory."[3] Jesus is unique, and in this sense he is final for us.

We may believe that Jesus is *the* son of God, while all of us are, or may become, children of God and joint heirs with Christ. "In Christ, God was reconciling the world to himself" (II Cor. 5:19 RSV). In Jesus' life, death, and resurrection we see the historical events by which God became more immanent in the world. There is no divine irruption from the outside. In their uniqueness, the events of the incarnation may be described as an eruption, an upsurging of the divine spirit of God. There is an incarnational principle at work through the cosmos, otherwise we could not speak of God being in us and we in God, and we see the exemplification of this divine principle in the events surrounding Jesus.

Certainly there was a change in the way human beings perceived God. We think of Yahweh and the plumb line of Amos; the forgiveness of Yahweh as perceived by Hosea; the power of suffering in the second Isaiah; the wisdom and virtue of God in the teachings of Socrates; heaven as a moral lawgiver as Confucius said; the control and even the elimination of desire in the thought

2. See Daniel Day Williams, *The Spirit and Forms of Love* (New York: Harper & Row, 1968), pp. 165–168.

3. R. D. Richardson, *The Gospel of Modernism* (London: Skeffington, 2nd ed., 1935), p. 177.

of the Buddha. Jesus, drawing solely from the Jewish tradition, brought many of these ideas together, but he also opened himself to God in such a way that a new impact was made on human history. There was a correlation between the subjective aim of God and Jesus' own aims that led to what we think of as a unity of the will, even though Jesus maintained the identity of his own will.

One could not predict from Jewish history, with its expectation of a messiah, that Jesus would appear. Indeed, the Jews have rejected the claim that Jesus is the messiah. But as Christians read history, something new had happened. There was real novelty, real mystery, real uniqueness in these events. It is said that the time was ripe for Jesus to appear; there was a historical readiness for novelty to emerge. We can speak of a revelation, a new level of consciousness, an awareness of God's grace or spirit at work. A new view of human relationships arose beside the older one and the two systems became rivals, and in spite of their kinship they separated. Thus a new age was born. Christians saw this as rooted in Jesus and they were filled with new energy by the gift of the Holy Spirit.[4]

Jesus was not only a channel for God's action, for his insights into the nature of God are equally important. Through Jesus' life and teachings, many persons have come and do come to knowledge of the reality of God and of his attributes. In one sense, we may claim that Jesus is the culmination of the process of revelation. Although we may purify details and change the metaphysical framework of our thinking, we come back to the basic attributes which Jesus taught.

Jesus taught with a certain kind of authority. All of us derive whatever authority we have from our own experience, reflection, and expertness, but we rely on some kind of consensus from those who share our perceptual attitudes. Jesus also derived his authority from his experience, and the disclosures that came to him were accepted by some of his hearers because these rang true in terms of

4. See Bernard Eugene Meland, *The Realities of Faith* (New York: Oxford University Press, 1962), pp. 257–266.

their intuitions and perceptions. He saw everything in relation to his sense of God's purpose for him. This did not make him reliable in terms of metaphysics, science, or history, but where God is at work through human beings he saw clearly what God was like and how persons could respond.[5] Thus we can claim that Jesus revealed *the* way of salvation, which is through unconditional commitment of the total self to the not fully known will of God.

It is important to remember that Jesus never claimed that we should worship him. Salvation comes from God, and through Jesus God worked to bring humankind into relations with God. Jesus was rightly called many names, which are really models by which we seek to understand him. Vincent Taylor finds forty-two such names for Jesus, among which the most important are: Christ, Son of Man, Lord, Son of God, King, Saviour, Mediator, Master.[6] And today some people speak of him as Liberator, Comrade, Exemplar. He was, as Peter Hamilton puts it, *sympathique* with God, by which he means that Jesus entered into God, as God entered into Jesus, even as we enter into each other when we are *sympathique,* and that God was *compatible* with Jesus, even as our friends are compatible with us, only this was a supreme instance of being *sympathique* and of being *compatible.*[7]

Another basis for Christology is the Logos doctrine of the Fourth Gospel. This usually offers us some difficulty, because we are not used to thinking in these terms. It is a more traditional phraseology than we have been using, but it points to God's word or God's aim for the world. We can believe that there was a consistency between God's aim and what Jesus did that was not identical but was remarkable. Thus, traditionally, "the Word became flesh." God has a generalized aim for all human beings, but we see a special content in the aim as Jesus realized it. Jesus had a vision of reality

5. See John B. Cobb, Jr., in *Process Philosophy and Christian Thought,* ed. Delwin Brown, Ralph E. James, Jr., and Gene Reeves (Indianapolis: Bobbs-Merrill Co., 1971), pp. 394–398.

6. See Vincent Taylor, *The Names of Jesus* (London: Macmillan & Co., Ltd., 1953).

7. Peter Hamilton, in *Christ for Us Today,* ed. Norman Pittenger (London: SCM Press, 1968), p. 163.

that we can capture for ourselves; this vision was of a future hope for the salvation of the world and also for God's reign in the world now.[8] In Whitehead's language, we can say that Jesus grasped at the fullness of God's meaning and purpose to the utmost; he "prehended" God and God "prehended" him. But God took the initiative, for God provided the original aim to which Jesus responded.

The problem is not that of how God could be in Jesus, for we believe that God as Holy Spirit indwells all humankind. It is the uniqueness of this presence in Jesus that is the paramount question, and this brings us back to his vision of God and the world. In Philippians we are told, "Let this mind be in you which was also in Christ Jesus" (Phil. 2:5,KJ) or "Have the same attitude Jesus Christ had" (G). Because of the life and death and resurrection of Jesus Christ, we are more capable of sharing that vision and therefore of aligning ourselves more nearly to God's aim for achieving an authentic humanity. Therefore, Christians claim that in Jesus God acted and was revealed more fully.

But even this is not enough to justify the belief that we are to accept Jesus as Lord and that we serve the living Christ. How we think of this depends on our interpretation of the resurrection. Although the resurrection is not open to empirical analysis, and only the Easter faith is accessible, we can speculate about the resurrection in terms of process theology. There is a distinction between "subjective" and "objective" immortality. If the "subject" lives on after death or is raised from death as a fully bodied human being, that is "subjective" immortality. But if what we are, think, and do is taken up into God, if God "prehends" the meaning of our lives, if we become, so to speak, part of God's everlasting "memory bank," that is "objective" immortality. If we find this meaningful, we may believe that the risen Christ is "objectively" immortal in God, and therefore can be prehended by us. From this perspective, says Peter Hamilton, "it is as meaningful to speak of Jesus raised in-

8. David R. Griffin, *A Process Christology* (Philadelphia: Westminster Press, 1973), pp. 155, 164, 203.

to God and 'living on' in God as it is to speak of God 'prehended' into and indwelling in—'living in'—Jesus. The first is the supreme instance of resurrection, the second the supreme instance of incarnation."[9]

This kind of talk is sheer speculation as to how it might have happened from the viewpoint of process thought, but the empirical evidence is that a new spiritual energy was released in Jesus' immediate followers as a result of the experience of resurrection. This new kind of life broke upon the little community in a radical way and was seen as the spirit of Jesus alive in their midst. The vividness of the sense of his presence did not last, however, and the ascension story is a way of closing out the resurrection appearances, to be followed by the gift of the Spirit at Pentecost. But the risen Christ remained available through the power of the Spirit to them and to us. Thus, to revert to process thought, we now can "prehend" the living Christ in the memory of God. The Logos which was in the historical Jesus is everlasting.

When those from a different theological perspective talk of "Jesus coming into my heart" or "I found Jesus" or "The spirit grasped me," they are pointing to the same reality. Jesus is made available to us when we "prehend" God from within the Christian tradition and we are changed, but most of us would probably prefer to use more traditional language, such as "I accept Jesus Christ as Lord and Savior" or "I was converted by the power of Jesus Christ." The empirical evidence of such faith always lies in its fruits, just as the disciples experienced the new creation of their lives through the resurrection. The transforming and creative power of God, a power available throughout the cosmos and throughout humankind, is seen as particularly available through faith in Jesus Christ. As Whitehead put it, "The essence of Christianity is the appeal to the life of Christ as a revelation of the nature of God and of his agency in the world."[10]

9. Hamilton, *Christ for Us Today*, p. 173.
10. Alfred North Whitehead, *Adventures of Ideas* (New York: Macmillan, 1933), p. 213.

This is our evaluation of Jesus in the light of the historical evidence, with some help from speculation about the *how* of the resurrection. Although our knowledge of the actual life of Jesus is limited by the inadequacy of our sources, the effect of Jesus upon his disciples and other followers and upon the coming generations leads us to conclude that never has another so nearly lived the life intended by God. Through him God was reconciling the world to God and God to the world!

## SALVATION THROUGH CHRIST

If the work of Jesus led men to greater service in the name of God, and if through the Logos dwelling in him God became more immanent in the world, Jesus is truly the savior. Traditional Christology has always put the emphasis on the saving work of Jesus' death and resurrection. We have put the emphasis both on his life and teachings and on the experience of him as available through the memory of God. Both are essential to an understanding of the effect of what is called the "atonement."

Historically, two things may be said. First, the death of Jesus and the resurrection experiences convinced the disciples of Jesus' messiahship and therefore let loose the energizing forces of God into the fellowship of the disciples. Second, the resurrection would have been impossible unless Jesus had made such an impression on his followers that the experience of the risen Christ became an unexpected and surprising sign that their faith had not been in vain. To some, the life and teachings leading to the crucifixion and resurrection have the greatest meaning for today; to others, the *sign* which verified the holiness of a life lived in the presence of God was more important than the life itself.

This, I think, is the reason for the stressing of the resurrection in the early church. It was the *sign* which indicated the truth of the claims of the early missionaries. They preached a "resurrection Christology" and soon the life of Jesus faded somewhat into the background. The whole development of theories of the atonement followed this line of thought, so that Jesus's death was thought of as some kind of a transaction between God and the devil or a vicarious payment for our sins. This line of thought was followed until the time of Peter Abelard, the heretical genius who brought forth the "moral theory" of the atonement. For Abelard, Christ's death was not a ransom to the devil or an infinite satisfaction for human sin. It was, rather, the supreme example of what it means to obey God; Jesus was seen as both the liberator and the exemplar.

> Alone thou goest forth, O Lord,
> In sacrifice to die;
> Is this thy sorrow naught to us
> Who pass unheeding by?
>
> Our sins, not thine, thou bearest, Lord,
> Make us thy sorrow feel,
> Till through our pity and our shame
> Love answers love's appeal.
>
> This is earth's darkest hour, but thou
> Dost light and life restore;
> Then let all praise be given thee
> Who livest evermore.
>
> Give us compassion for thee, Lord,
> That, as we share this hour,
> Thy cross may bring us to thy joy
> And resurrection power.[11]

The complete work of Christ means the opening of the door of God's power and sustaining strength to all who follow in his train. There is a *movement* of redemption that began then. The Logos

11. Peter Abelard, tr. F. Bland Tucker, *The Hymnal 1940* (New York: Church Pension Fund, 1940, 1943), No. 68.

working in the man Jesus is the true Christ, who was made available as never before through the work of Jesus.

To know Christ is in a real sense to know God. It is obvious that many have come to a knowledge of the fullness of the love of God through traditions and religions that do not know Jesus as the Christ; that is what we would expect if we understand God's presence in the world as a redeeming and loving reality. For Christians, however, we see in Jesus Christ a unique offering of God to us. "In Jesus Christ," wrote Daniel Day Williams, "God has given what is needed to heal the disorders in the human spirit, and to inaugurate a new possibility for every life. Human history, and indeed the history of the whole creation, can now be understood from the perspective created by this action of God in Jesus."[12] Once a person is committed to living according to the way revealed in Jesus Christ, one is on the road to salvation. It is the atonement which is the supreme lesson, that victory comes through absolute commitment to a righteous and loving God, by whose grace we are brought from Christ to the kingdom. Repent, therefore, and turn from the powers of evil to the powers of God, from the sins of desire to the aspirations of love, from life as it is to life as it may become, that the rule of God may be realized on earth and God's aim be fulfilled here as it is in God's innermost being.

## PURIFICATION THROUGH CHRIST

All religions tend to add dangerous accretions as they develop. Most religions have no way of purifying themselves. As Christianity spread from culture to culture it took on the coloration of those cultures, sometimes adopting philosophical concepts that were not consistent with the original position, or the political models for God of the Greeks and Romans in place of the suffering love model, or the liturgical contaminations drawn from pagan

12. *The Spirit and Forms of Love* (New York: Harper & Row, 1968), p. 155.

rites, or the ethical views and mores of a given group which had become dominant. This could lead to beliefs, positions, and actions that seem inconsistent with the basic teachings of the earliest church.

Christianity has been self-renewing when it has held itself accountable primarily to the life and teachings of Jesus in the synoptic record. When he has been forgotten, the church has become the least Christ-like. The church has been able at times to transcend its foibles and weaknesses whenever there has been a revival of interest in Jesus, who has a purifying effect on those who attempt to see their lives through his eyes. They become *sympathique* with Jesus as he is *sympathique* with God.

In the Gospels we read of this purifying effect of Jesus on those who came into contact with him. He could see through people to their innermost being, and they knew he knew their secret. We recall the stories of the Samaritan woman at the well with many husbands, the paralytic who is healed, the crazy person out of whom demons are cast, the tax collector who offered to reform. It was a physical and spiritual tonic to be in his presence, although it was also threatening to one's old way of life.

Those who are confronted by Jesus today experience this same purifying effect. We have already explained how we think Jesus is present as the living Christ; we need to remember that the content of this living presence is found in the record of Jesus' life and teachings. So we measure ourselves in the light of the fundamental attitudes and teachings of Jesus. We come to share and participate in his vision of reality. Thus, we are challenged and purified by the reality of God that stands behind this model of God as found in Jesus. The purifying effect of Jesus has been likened to fire, because fire purifies as it burns. John the Baptist promised that the coming one would baptize with water and with fire, and both are cleansing and both can destroy. There is a separation of wheat from the chaff. We do stand under judgment. We can come to ourselves and turn to God. It is simply a fact of experience that this happens to people when they are confronted with the power revealed through Jesus Christ.

## The Challenge of Christ

We have said much about turning back to Jesus. In doing so, we find perspective, salvation, and purification. The story is not complete if we stop here, however. Christianity is a religion of discipleship and community. Its motto should not be "Back to Jesus" but "Forward with Christ." "Christ is the one and necessary mediator. . . . He leads; we follow. He redeems; we are redeemed. . . . Our hope is that we may be as Jesus, not that we may be Christs."[13] "What think ye of Christ?" is still the key question for Christians; it both divides and unites them. Today, we are searching for new concepts and models by which to restore the kernel of this faith without the accretions of the ages.

When we read the Gospels, when we open ourselves to the power of love revealed in Christ, when we meditate upon his courage, his love, his faithfulness, his winsomeness, the challenge is there. It is a challenge to turn from our habitual activities, to open ourselves to the liberation and freedom of all humankind, to ground ourselves in the growing good so that we may become agents of a God whose aim is the well-being of all creatures. This challenge faces our total being, and asks for the commitment of that total self to the God and Father of Jesus Christ. We entrust ourselves to the God Jesus trusted; we accept the aim of the God Jesus aligned his aim with; we seek the rule of the God Jesus announced; and we do all of this because of the challenge which Jesus presents to those of us who have freedom to respond.

## Jesus and God

We have said that in understanding and accepting Jesus we understand and accept the Christian God. But Jesus is not God; that is a form of heresy as well as nonsense if we start with Jesus' humanity. It was not God who died on the cross; it was Jesus of

---

13. William Temple, ed., *Doctrine in the Church of England* (New York: Macmillan, 1938), p. 78.

Nazareth, the Galilean carpenter, the son of Joseph and Mary. The early church fathers made this distinction in a different way. They simply insisted that God could not suffer or change. But we would turn it the other way, so that although God did not die when Jesus was crucified, God suffered with him and shared his suffering, prehending Jesus' experience and transforming it so that it became a potentiality for new life.

Using traditional trinitarian language, we may say that God as Father is the transcendent power who is the unchanging source of values; as Father, God is primordial and everlasting, the source of creativity and potentiality, and it is God's aim to which we seek to align ourselves. God as Logos is the Word, that mode through which God is revealed to us; the human personality of Jesus was the point at which the Logos became uniquely ingredient in the world, so that we can say that Jesus' human aim and the aim of God freely came into union. God as Spirit is the indwelling of God as consequent in our natures, giving us both life and hope. This keeps the essential meaning of God as Trinity, for the three aspects of God should be conceived as three "faces" or "modes" or "masks." We have three aspects of a single process or actual entity. Only in Jesus of Nazareth, Christians believe, is the second face revealed clearly, so that we have knowledge of a dipolar God, who is both primordial and consequent, both abstract and concrete, both transcendent and immanent, and by turning to Jesus in his life, death, and resurrection we see the full activity of the Logos.

There is a warning in *Doctrine in the Church of England* which must be kept in mind: "It is always to be remembered that the religious value of the incarnation consists primarily in what it declares concerning God rather than in what it claims for the historic Jesus, while yet it is *through* faith in Jesus Christ that [believers] were led to the Christian's knowledge of God. They saw 'the light of the knowledge of the glory of God in the face of Jesus Christ.' "[14] We believe in the method of observation and reason.

14. Ibid., p. 76.

Surely we, too, can see now more clearly the face of Jesus Christ, and in that face there is "the light of the knowledge of the glory of God." We place Jesus as a model for God within the wider scope of other ways of thinking about God, for God works through the cosmos and through nature, impersonally and personally, and through society and human nature. The God of Jesus Christ is our God.

# 7
# *Why Believe in the Church?*

The church faces a challenge today which it has not known since before the time of Constantine. Except in a few lands, the church carries little influence and in some it is opposed by the state. No longer is it considered essential to the social structure. It has been accused of being on the side of privilege, of being against those in lower classes of society, of participating in racial and sexist prejudice, and of opposing most revolutionary and liberating movements. There have been some exceptions to these charges, but often only at the level of the World Council of Churches or among certain church leaders.

Yet, if Christianity is still a meaningful form of living, if it is charged with responsibility to align itself with God's aims for the world, and if it contains a message of salvation for humankind, it needs to be formed as a community with some kind of power and influence. Although no particular form of the church is sacrosanct, some form of organization is necessary for survival. There is a place in human living for a social organism which will promote Christian living. Those who have chosen to follow Jesus Christ need a church.

### JESUS AND THE CHURCH

I believe that it is amply verified that Jesus did not intend to found a church. He neither foresaw nor desired the institution which bears his name. The resurrection experiences started a new social movement drawn from Jesus' immediate followers, and this led to a Jewish sect which soon became the church. As Alfred Loisy said, "What Jesus announced was the kingdom of God; what came was the Catholic Church."[1] But that process did not take place immediately. The little band of Jewish Christians in Jerusalem continued to worship with their fellow Jews, and the only difference, howbeit the important one, was their attitude toward Jesus as risen Lord, whom they *now* believed to be the messiah.

The life and teachings of Jesus might never have resulted in a church, except for the resurrection experience. The little, enthusiastic band of disciples, basing its teachings probably on the sermon of Peter as reported in Acts (10:34–43), soon had a considerable following. As the movement spread, not only Greek-speaking Jews but Greek pagans quickly joined the group, which had become bilingual. Greek ideas began to permeate the inherited Jewish thinking. Yet we need to understand that the church was part of the Christ event, although the historical development centered in what seemed to be fortuitous occasions. In one sense the church was a consequence of a series of events; in another it was the culmination of all that had happened.

From the beginning, Christianity was a mystery-cult in its own right, emphasizing the idea of a dying and rising deity, and believing, in the words of Peter, that "every one who believes in him shall receive remission of sins through his name" (Acts 10:43 RSV). The emphasis on the death and resurrection and on the remission of sins was very close to the Greek mysteries. But the earliest Christians remained within Judaism and conceived of themselves as "the new Israel" until Paul's Gentile group became powerful. Through Paul's influence, Christianity became a church that could not stay within Judaism, and the church became a rival both to Judaism and to the mystery-cults. The final death blow to Jewish Christianity

1. Cited by Frederick C. Grant, *Anglican Theological Review*, XXI, p. 191. See Bernard Lee, *The Becoming of the Church* (New York: Paulist, 1974), pp. 285–286.

came when James, the brother of Jesus and the leader of the Jewish Christians in Jerusalem, was martyred.

Paul might well be called the first churchman. Not only have his teachings influenced the church more than those of any other leader, but Paul's power of evangelizing and organizing did much to establish the church as an independent body throughout the known world. The origins of Christian orthodoxy probably centered more in Paul than in Jesus. Even if this be true, however, we must not underestimate the importance of other Christians, known and unknown, both men and women, who participated in this leadership. Paul was merely the headliner, who soon overshadowed James, Peter, Barnabas, Mark, Priscilla, Phoebe, and the others. His influence has been more permanent, perhaps too much so according to some, because of his writings.

Although it can be said with some assurance that Jesus did not intend to found the church, and although Paul and some of the other leaders had more to do with its development, it is equally true that *without Jesus there would be no church.* He was the cornerstone, and faith in Jesus as risen Lord was the central commitment. Implicit in the life and work of Jesus (unless lost to the world entirely) was the necessity for breaking away from Judaism and for the development of a new tradition and community.

Jesus was a typical Jew, but there was much of prophetic radicalism in his teaching and living which could not be palatable to the orthodox Jews (or to the orthodox anywhere). He rejected fasting; he broke the laws of the Sabbath at a time when there was rigid observance; he ignored the food laws, thus striking at the heart of the Mosaic distinction between clean and unclean foods; he always placed human need above formalism, even when there was no outstanding reason for doing so; he carried the concept of a living God to the point where God seeks erring children, whether they pay attention to ceremonial law or not; and he insisted that there would be an uncomfortably imminent fulfilling of the messianic hopes. Above all, there seemed to be an authority in Jesus' teachings and healing that imperiled the sanctions of the organized groups.

Jesus never consciously broke with Judaism and usually observed its forms and practices; but his radicalism not only brought about enmity for himself, it also made it inevitable that sooner or later any movement bearing his name should be declared anathema. With this as a background, and with the universal appeal implicit in his message, it was not long before the little Jewish-Christian group found itself outside the pale of organized Judaism. In all of this, the spirit of Jesus permeated the group; they had the beginning of "the mind of Christ," and they were on their way to turning the world upside down.

## An Evolving Church

Jewish opposition to the Christians grew rapidly, and this is already reflected in the Gospels themselves. By the time of the Fourth Gospel, Christianity was struggling for its independent existence. This unknown writer saw the church as a spiritual fellowship, withdrawn from the world, working under the guidance of the supernatural and mystical Logos-Christ. Even the love expressed in this Gospel is restricted to the fellowship. The attitude toward "the Jews" is one of enmity.

The development of the early church was accompanied by a great variety of practice and belief. There was freedom to experiment, and many practices were tried and discarded. There were no prescriptions, no set beliefs, and every group developed its own cultus. At the same time, within this variety was a real and sound unity. There was room for difference of opinion on many subjects, as long as one believed in Jesus Christ. He was the cornerstone of the early church, and his name was the name above all others. In spite of some of the excesses of the early church, of the enthusiasm that was so great that the apostles were accused of being drunk before nine in the morning (Acts 2:13–15), of the speaking with tongues and other ecstasies, there was a fundamental soundness in the early church because it had been founded in the spirit of Jesus of Nazareth.

Modern communions have sought a sanction for their forms of church government in the New Testament, and they can find almost any except the papal. We know that the earliest leaders were called "apostles" or "elders," but these terms had no distinctive meaning, except that the apostles were those who witnessed the resurrection, as Paul did. From them grew a diversity of overlapping offices: "apostles, prophets, teachers, evangelists, workers of miracles, healers, shepherds, rulers, bishops, deacons."[2] There were some women among them. Gradually out of the chaos came some semblance of order. About the beginning of the second century the ministry began to be systematized, with the presbyter-bishop at the center. Some churches were still headed by councils of elders or prophets. Only later did the monarchial bishop evolve. In time, the threefold order of bishops, priests, and deacons became dominant. They were servants of God and of the laity, for the church was thought of as the people of God, not of clergy as first-class and laity as second-class citizens.

There were two sacraments from the earliest time. It is hard to know when baptism was accepted as a basic rite, but probably it was part of the church's evangelistic effort. From the beginning Jesus did not baptize, and Paul did not consider it a major part of his ministry. It probably goes back to the "baptism which John preached" and so has its roots in Judaism. The tradition that Jesus was baptized by John was a model for the early church. By the time the Gospels were written, baptism was the accepted rite of initiation, and there is an interpolation at the conclusion of the Gospel of Matthew telling the disciples to baptize in the name of the Trinity; the date of this addition is uncertain, but surely before 80 A.D.

---

2. Grant, *Anglican Theological Review*, p. 196.

Although the earliest traditions concerning the Last Supper seem to indicate messianic expectation, and the earliest form of the ceremony was a fellowship meal, it soon developed, probably under Paul's direction, into a memorial of Jesus' death. By the time Mark was written, the Pauline influence of I Corinthians 11:17–34 may have become the dominant one. It is likely that the Lukan form is the more primitive one, and this view is supported in Acts, partially in Mark and Matthew, and in the early practice of the Corinthian church.[3] The meal was repeated regularly, and soon included the sense of fellowship with the risen Lord. From this point, it is not hard to understand how the present form of communion service evolved. After the communion was separated from the evening meal or love feast, it was changed into a more formalized liturgy that developed over the next centuries.

There is reference to the "breaking of bread" in Acts, but the earliest worship in the Jerusalem church was probably a continuation of its regular Jewish practices of participation in the worship in the synagogues and temples, supplemented by private meetings for the supper, prayer, and reading of Scripture (the Jewish Bible). The Gentile Church was cut off from the Jewish-Christian community from the beginning, and it met primarily in private houses and secluded places. There were hymns and recitations of Jesus' words, parables, and incidents of his ministry. As the church's liturgy developed, the more informal services dropped into the background, and finally the mass became the norm.

The church of the New Testament and the early fathers was an evolving church, developing on a hit-or-miss basis and meeting the changing needs as they appeared. This is true not only of the ministry and sacraments but of creeds, canon of Scripture, and doctrine. The threefold ministry did develop. No matter what Jesus said about being a rock, the fact remains that Peter, like James and Paul, was only one of the leaders, and the church was not founded on him. As the church grew, it added important elements from its

3. Ernest W. Parsons, *The Religion of the New Testament* (New York: Harper & Row, 1939), pp. 28–30.

pagan surroundings, especially from Greek philosophy and the Roman sense for order and constitutional law. As a faith, cult, sect, body of belief, and worshipping fellowship, the early church met and mastered its human situations, often by compromise but many times by standing upright in the midst of oppression even unto the death of its martyrs. The church through the centuries has not always been true to its trust, but it has been a dominant factor in the development of Western culture and at its best has deserved its title as "the body of Christ."

The early church was recognized for what it accomplished, and many images or models were used to describe it. Some of these images no longer appeal to our imagination, but others are still relevant, such as people of God, *ekklesia* (those who are called out), *koinonia* (sharers of a gift), body of Christ, followers of the way, the new covenant.[4] All barriers between persons were broken down, so that "there is neither Jew nor Greek, there is neither slave nor free, there is neither male nor female; for you are all one in Christ Jesus" (Gal. 3:28, RSV).

## WHAT THE CHURCH IS

An empirical analysis of what the church is must begin with a description of what the church does, with full cognizance of what the church does not do, and with recognition that the empirical church stands under the judgment of its New Testament images or models. The church today has met with many setbacks. It is oppressed in all communist countries; its work is limited by civil authorities in some areas; and it is simply ignored by governments in others. As long ago as 1933, Alfred North Whitehead wrote that "its dogmas no longer dominate: its divisions no longer interest: its

4. See my *Christian Nurture and the Church* (New York: Charles Scribner's Sons, 1961), pp. 4–15; Colin Williams, *The Church: New Directions in Theology*, Vol. IV (Philadelphia: Westminster Press, 1968), pp. 58–64; Paul S. Minear, *Images of the Church in the New Testament* (Philadelphia: Westminster Press, 1960).

institutions no longer direct the patterns of life."[5] There has been a drastic decline in the support of foreign missions, and there have been grievous deficits in the budgets of the denominations. When the churches have sought to influence social action, civil rights, racial justice, and foreign affairs of our government, their own people have withdrawn their financial and moral support. There is a kind of spiritual introversion which stresses the comforting of church people and ignores the challenge of the prophetic notes of the Gospel. The gap between modern scholarship and the information available to the normal lay person has undercut the church's reputation for integrity and honesty in teaching. The education of the youth of the church has dropped off amazingly in spite of the search of the younger generation for religious roots. There is nothing to distinguish the church from the material world, the Christian from the pagan.

In some ways, the church has attempted to put its own house in order through its leadership. The missionary programs of the main line churches are no longer conceived in terms of white supremacy or political maneuvering, and in most cases there is within the missionary effort a humility that treats others as equals. Where workers are desired by churches in developing fields, they go as equals with the local leaders and serve under them. The divisions between churches are breaking down, and there are some mergers that cross traditional barriers of the nature of ministry and church, with the Church of South India as one of the first and best examples. There are councils of churches at all geographical levels, and in some cases local councils now include both Catholics and Protestants (and in some rare cases the councils are interfaith and include Jews). At national levels there are many effective councils for cooperation between churches, as in the National Council of Churches in the United States. There are councils to cover continents or large areas in Africa, Asia, and elsewhere. Topping all this is the success of the World Council of Churches in bringing

5. *Adventures of Ideas* (New York: Macmillan, 1933), p. 205.

Protestant and Orthodox groups together from every country in the world, and with Roman Catholic cooperation at many levels. Within the churches, there is opposition to such developments, and especially to the social and political significance of this kind of cooperation, but there is also wide support.

The same thing may be said about the spectacular developments in scholarship. The ways in which the Bible has been studied in the past century are slowly being passed on to lay people. Many of them have followed the theological controversies surrounding the death-of-God movement and the rediscoveries of the reality and nature of God in terms of a modern world view. The experiments in worship have led to both disarray and reconstruction of liturgical practices and meanings. Ethical and moral values, at first threatened by revolutionary upheavals, are now being seen in a clearer light. In spite of the lowering of morale in religious education, new practices are emerging that support free discussion of religious issues. Although the churches are still muddled or divided over social issues, the new consciousness of social responsibility among conservatives is a promising development. Certainly the church is far from being a spiritual luxury.

Church members are likely to be aware of the failings of the church, for they are caught up in its pettiness and faithlessness. But they still see the church as a basis for hope that under God a baffled and needy world will move toward liberation, for the recognition of the worth of all persons, and for the acceptance of God's sovereignty in terms of what we conceive to be God's aim for humankind. In spite of its weaknesses, the church is the agent for the mission of Jesus Christ. When Paul wrote that the church is the Body of Christ, he meant that the work begun by Jesus Christ, as mediator, as revealer, as savior, should rest in the church.

There is no such thing as a single empirical church. The church of human experience is made up of many denominations. For example, there are about 275 churches from about 90 countries in the World Council of Churches, and there are more than that outside the cooperative movements or in rival ones. All claim to be part of the universal church, and as a fact of experience they perform most of the functions which make the name Christian applicable. The divisions within Christendom are such that there is no single organism; rather, there are several major groupings and many minor ones with different beliefs, practices, and functions. These divisions are hard to heal because points of difference are often held as matters of *revealed truth* rather than as empirical knowledge. If a person is convinced that the only valid baptism is by immersion, or the only valid sacrament of the Lord's Supper requires wine of a specific alcoholic content or a certain type of ministry, the appeal to the efficacy of other customs and practices is not likely to be convincing.

When we say that we believe in one, holy, catholic, and apostolic church, we are in one way expressing a pious hope or belief in an unrealized ideal. Yet the churches do express their oneness, especially those who cooperate in the World Council of Churches or enter into dialogue with each other in cooperative enterprises. They do exhibit some degree of being holy, in that they are set apart for certain tasks, especially the worship of a holy God. Insofar as the church deals with the brokenness of the world and seeks to have a ministry of healing, liberation, and reconciliation, it is catholic. The church is apostolic when it shares in the apostolic mission and there is some continuity between the intention of the church today and that of the original apostolate. The church, then, is in process toward such goals as these marks indicate, rather than being one, holy, catholic, and apostolic.

There are two elements present in every church: faith in Christ, and knowledge of the Scriptures. There may be wide latitude of belief in both areas, but the church which does not provide these two aspects of Christianity as central may be considered at the periphery or outside the boundaries of the Christian Church. The practice of baptism and the Lord's Supper are also considered central by most churches, but the Society of Friends is an exception.

The church must be a worshipping church. It must provide for Christian fellowship. It must give instruction in the beliefs of the church, including the Bible, interpretations of God's aims for individuals and for society, the meaning and function of values in the world, and the place of religious living in the whole of life. It must provide a real pastoral relationship, helping persons to achieve the potential of their spiritual and human development, making suffering endurable when necessary, and administering to the general needs of the people. It must keep alive the missionary spirit, taking the good news of the Gospel to all nations, and interpreting the church's hopes for the world to those on the outside. It must continue to have no national boundaries, working toward an international order of good will.

The church has not consistently achieved any of these norms, but it has functioned in all of these areas, working as God's agent of salvation and liberation for all people and for society as a whole. The church as a social institution will live or die on the basis of its performance. Throughout its history, it has had times of internal corruption, ineptitude, and indifference, but it has managed to be a real conserver of values and of civilization in the world's darkest hours.

*The Christian church is a worshipping community.* It has many different ways of worshipping, through the sacraments, through prayer meetings, through formal and informal ceremonial, through preaching and the reading of Scripture, and through Quaker quiet periods. Worship is the recognition of the mystery which lies at the heart of reality. It is an offering of the self in complete commitment to a God of suffering love, whose aim for humankind is a society in which those aims are sovereign. There is the unseen touch of God, which gives us perspective, courage, and power. The act of worship lifts us to the presence of God and at the same time strengthens us to do what we perceive to be God's will. It is a love relationship.

When we go to church, we expect to meet God there, although God meets us everywhere. In the church's worship we meet God with others who have the same purpose. Thus, each of us derives strength from the fact that our fellow worshippers are doing something very similar, and we become aware that we are part of a corporate body prehending God together and also at least unconsciously prehending each other. These simultaneous prehensions strengthen all the members of a group, just as they do at a political rally or football games, except that the focus is on God. This common focus increases our devotion to values, so that we are enabled to align our aims with God's aims. Thus, we not only cooperate in our worship but there is the potential of activity in other areas as we face the moral, social, and political problems of daily life.

The church has not always provided the high level of worship which is essential to Christianity at its best. It is possible to cheapen worship, so that it appeals to our baser motives. But even ill-conceived formulas for worship do not necessarily block God's presence from us. Although we can worship God outside the church or the community of believers, it is not likely that we will do so. The church provides the time, place, opportunity, and intention to worship. As Whitehead wrote, "The power of God is the worship he inspires."[6]

*The church provides fellowship.* Christians of an earlier day, coming to Rome as strangers, could always be assured of welcome by their fellow believers. Today this is still true to some extent in all lands, because Christianity provides a fellowship which transcends the barriers of race, sex, or nation. This is probably more true among the younger churches than at home, where fellowship is often limited to the denomination or groups within the denomination. There can be genuine fellowship (*koinonia,* sharing) in common worship, church suppers, cooperative activities of service and witness, and it reaches its height for many in the service of Holy Communion. Group actions within particular congregations and in common activities of larger groups increase the sense of a shared devotion to a common cause. This fellowship sometimes results in

6. Alfred North Whitehead, *Science and the Modern World* (New York: Macmillan, 1925), p. 276.

a group consciousness, a sense of mutual strengthening and sharing in the "way" of Christian living. No person alone can do much to work for the coming of the kingdom, but the mutual resources of many persons dedicated to the same cause have accomplished wonders.

While organization is part of the necessary means for the church to do its work, no ecclesiasticism or polity is ever final. The church is primarily *a fellowship of the spirit,* and just because it is essentially a free fellowship it is open to divisions. Even the goal of fellowship is rarely achieved today, but insofar as the church does express this fellowship in Christ's spirit, it holds the promise of a new order for humankind.

This community of the Holy Spirit also has an effect on the lives of those who are members. Within the interpersonal relationships of the fellowship or community, relations are strained and then restored; alienation is followed by reconciliation; sin is followed by forgiveness; and no matter how much relations are strained there is a message that individuals are accepted as they are. The members do not approve of each other, but they accept each other, and thus they are free to accept God's grace and be transformed. Fellowship may start at the coffee-hour sociability level, but it often moves to the depths of human pain and alienation and then becomes the channel of God's healing power.[7]

*The church provides for teaching and learning.* The church has a serious responsibility to care for and nurture the minds and spirits of its members through preaching, teaching, and an overall program of education. This includes making available the printed word, audiovisual media, and other educational resources. The church needs to organize the results of its best thinking and to make this available at all levels. The doctrines of the church must be as free from error as possible. It is truth that makes people free,

---

7. See my *Christian Nurture and the Church,* pp. 119–134.

and thus truth must be sought with all the cooperating intelligences available to the church. When asked, "What *can* we believe?" the church must have replies that are satisfactory in terms of modern ways of thinking about the nature of reality. Recent developments in theology give promise of meeting this need. The church presents the Bible as central to its thought, but it needs to be made clear how we are to think in biblical language and thought forms, so that they may be related to the way we think today. As we learn to use the Bible critically and appreciatively, we find resources for understanding its meaning for creative living as Christians. The church seeks to interpret the will of God, without interfering with the freedom of conscience of its members. The aim of God for this world needs to be grasped and understood, and this is a difficult task. In both its teaching and its pastoral ministry, the way we understand the place of God in human lives is of paramount importance. The will of God, which is the utmost growth of good for individuals and for society, is held before Christian believers as an ideal, and when backed by interpretation and instruction people in some instances may apply this general aim to the particulars of their own lives. The church sees God's will working independently of human purpose and desires as a growth of meaning and value in this world, and as we become aware of values as an ongoing process of divine and human relationships, we may be brought more nearly into the stream of divine life. Finally, the church teaches that religion applies to the whole of life. God requires the allegiance of the total person, for there is no activity of human beings which should be free from the aims of God. The destiny of humankind is to come under the sovereignty or rule or kingdom of God, and this involves the purifying of the present social, political, and economic order through the activity of human beings. This is the church's challenge to the world, and we must meet the conditions of this challenge or face the consequences in terms of suffering, war, and perhaps the end of this civilization.

It is obvious that groups within the church do not agree on the details of these teaching functions or on the content which should be included. But the basic resources for such teaching go back to the record of Jesus' teachings and the total biblical message. We know enough about ways of learning to be modest about hopes for agreement even about the facts, but there can be greater unity of mind and spirit in the seeking of a common life together which recognizes the worth of persons in God's sight. The church's task is to seek *unity of spirit* where there cannot be intellectual unity or organic union of churches. The shared commitment is where certitude lies and cooperation becomes possible, although the search for assertions that are true must go on.

Education is all of this and more. It is initiation into a way of thinking as Christians, being absorbed in the sources and the traditions; it is also the gaining of the skills and tools whereby we can appropriate what the church offers. But unless we help learners develop the art of thinking for themselves, most of what we do will be indoctrination and their beliefs will remain secondhand ones. So we need to help people to think straight, which is not an easy task. We need to help them explore the data, interpret their meanings, and come to conclusions concerning their beliefs, to go through, in other words, the process illustrated in this book. But in the process there will be new disclosures, new ways of looking on things, new realizations of what it means to be a Christian today, which in turn will have to be tested for meaning, coherence, and consistency.

*The church has a pastoral function.* This function has appeared most significantly on the frontiers of the church, through the works of hospitals, schools, and general deeds of charity. From the beginning, Christians were known as those who cared for each other, for widows and orphans, the poor, the sick and afflicted. There can be no doubt of the influence of the parable of the Good Samaritan on the church. The church has ministered to groups and to individuals, helping persons to realize their potentialities for achieving values in their lives. The confessional, pastoral counseling, and the sacraments have been aimed at the overcoming of alienation and the achievement of moral and spiritual integrity. People have been enabled to face suffering with courage, to overcome personal and social obstacles, to regain health, morale, and stability, to make life eminently worthwhile. Bernard Meland speaks of living "upon the grace of one another."[8]

The role of the pastor in the church today is clearly outlined in terms of visiting the sick, counseling the confused, comforting the sorrowing, aiding those in financial distress, assisting those preparing for marriage or baptism or confirmation, placing families within the helping hands of social agencies, referring the mentally ill to the proper professionals, and ministering to the dying. Of course, lay persons also do these things in the name of Christ, but the trained clergy have resources of expertness that are valuable, just as trained lay people do. The only healing power is the power of God, and the pastor (as well as the doctor) brings these healing gifts to those who call for them. Thus God releases us from the bondage of fear and anxiety into the freedom which comes to those who love God.

*The church has a mission to the whole world.* It is a paradox of the effectiveness of the church that when it is devoted to the spread of the Christian message among others its home bases maintain the highest degree of health. Missions have been under a cloud of suspicion because of the misguided zeal of some missionaries, because of confusion concerning the effects of missionary endeavors when mixed with enculturation from the sending country, and because of the influence of imperialistic forces on the receiving culture. Furthermore, those who were supporting missions withdrew their support because of a new philosophy that granted some integrity to the receiving culture and its religious heritage. Today, the strongest missionary efforts are maintained by conservative groups who stick pretty much to the older methods. A perusal of any modern book on missions, however, will convince even skeptical

8. Bernard E. Meland, *Faith and Culture* (New York: Oxford University Press, 1953), p. 177.

readers that the new approach, while not as spectacular, is more sound in its understanding of the language, customs, culture, and religion of the receiving group; furthermore, the relations with the newer churches have remained healthy because most imperialism has vanished, although the need for money for the newer churches puts them at a disadvantage in making their own decisions.

If Christianity is worth anything, it is worth giving away to all who will accept it. The churches that have come to maturity in the former mission fields are now supplying leadership for the world church and are making strong witnesses in their own countries. Christianity is an *expanding* religion, and it claims the world as its field. It is not wedded to Western civilization any more than it was wedded to Palestine, and indigenous churches everywhere are becoming the nuclei of hope in many countries. There have been setbacks as emerging nations become suspicious of what they think of as a Western import, and in some areas growth will be slow. We are just beginning to learn how to participate in dialogue with Muslims, Hindus, Buddhists, and others of the world religions. But the religious motif runs deep in all cultures, and there is hope for the future.

*The church is ecumenical and international in scope.* This follows naturally from a consideration of the church's missionary outlook. As Edgar S. Brightman wrote before World War II, "Feeble as the Church's power has been in preserving world peace, no one should forget that the Church is the only permanent institution making for friendly cooperation between nations, and also the only institution which by right is in a position to rebuke the state or to point at a king with the words, 'Thou art the man.' "[9] The church by itself rarely stops evil, but persons nurtured by the church frequently become leaders for social betterment, including international relations.

9. Edgar S. Brightman, in *Theology and Modern Life: Essays in Honor of Harris Franklin Rall*, ed. Paul Schilpp (Chicago: Willett, Clark, 1940), p. 269.

Those whose hopes were raised first by the League of Nations and then by the United Nations, only to have those hopes dashed, can see a similarity in the developments among the churches. Slowly there has come into being the World Council of Churches, at first run pretty much by American and European types but with a broad sympathy for other cultures. But the situation changed, and those from less developed areas became leaders within the council. At the conferences on world and national issues, those from the so-called Third World were heard. And their view of what was needed was different from the views of their European and North American friends. The demand of the churches for a critical consciousness in relation to human need plays a significant role in the mission of ecumenical Christianity to the whole world. This raises the hopes of the downtrodden majority of all people for freedom from oppression and poverty, which is an essential part of the gospel story. Those in power in the more privileged churches do not yet see clearly what their responsibility is, and thus there is tension among the members, especially those whose positions are threatened by the rise of the oppressed among us. Thus, the fact that there is a World Council of Churches which is able to mediate between the churches from depressed areas and those in more fortunate circumstances is an important element in the unity in Christ signified by the ecumenical movement.

## THE CHURCH AND THE PEOPLE OF TODAY

When we begin to understand what the church is and what its opportunities are, we can believe in the church. Because the church for its efficiency depends on fallible human beings, a particular congregation in a location in a given town may not meet the standards or arouse the interests we hold. That does not excuse us from seeking other parishes until we find one that does challenge us. When we see that the church is *not simply* a dispenser of sacraments, of assurance, and of grace, to be called on for baptisms, weddings, and funerals, and to be attended on Christmas and Easter, we may be surprised.

The church is an organization of numerous believers and groups of believers, which continues Christ's work in the world by making people more sensitive to God through its various functions. The church accomplishes many things. There is no ideal church in our experience, but there are fallible churches constituted of those who wish to be committed (with whatever reservations) to God's aims for us. None of us lives a fully Christian life without its worship, its sense of being a community of the Holy Spirit, its teaching, its pastoral aids, its missionary vision, and its worldwide and inclusive perspective. The church is the Body of Christ, and all denominations are members of that Body.

The church's spiritual and moral effectiveness is hindered by its divisions. One does not need to plead for the organic unity of all the churches, but surely the ecumenical movement holds out the hope that all Christians eventually will recognize the validity of the efforts of other Christians. There is no supernatural sanction for one type of worship, one kind of ministry, or one theory of the sacraments. The proper measure of any of these things is their spiritual efficiency. Until there is this common recognition, no one's worship is complete, no one denomination can claim that its ministry is valid, no one communion can offer a fully valid sacrament, and there can be no truly catholic church. For until worship, ministry, and sacrament are fully available to all qualified members of the universal church, our actions are limited in their effects, and therefore they are only partially valid. The church must heal its own wounds before it can be aligned with the aims of God with anything approaching a single mind. The church is a means for the doing of God's will, it is the embodiment of the work of Christ, and it is the teacher of spiritual and moral values, but a divided church cannot do these things adequately. There is hope, therefore, in the ecumenical movement.

We *can* believe in the church, because it is the only organization in the world which stands for the achievement of the wholeness of human beings, for the achievement of spiritual and moral values, and for the relations between individuals and nations which is a foretaste of the hoped-for coming of God's sovereignty in the world. Furthermore, it is hard to be a Christian or acquire the values of the Christian tradition outside the church. As John F. Scott wrote: "People say they can live moral lives without Christ and the church. And of course that is true! But they ought to realize that in so doing they are living on the accumulated religious capital of past generations. It is the spiritual contributions of our [forebears] that have lifted our civilization to its present level. And when we become content just to live off those accumulated resources *without making any new spiritual investment with our own lives,* we are walking on pretty dangerous ground. It is like inheriting a trust fund and squandering the capital. The church needs, and the world needs, men and women who will give of themselves to maintaining and increasing the spiritual deposit of which the church is the custodian, instead of just sitting back and dissipating what others have created."[10]

The church has fared badly at the hands of modern, intelligent, religious men and women, because they have not realized the social implications, the spiritual indebtedness, and the moral requirements of their Christian beliefs. These responsibilities can best be met within the community of the life of the church at its best, and both the individual and the church can be mutually supported and improved by dedicated and intelligent service in the church of Jesus Christ.

10. Editorial in *The Pacific Churchman*, May, 1940, p. 3.

# 8
# *On Being Human*

It would be pleasant to believe, in Harry Stack Sullivan's phrase, that we are "much more simply human than otherwise." Each of us is a society, made up of many processes which are becoming and perishing, and we are parts of a larger society that ultimately includes the whole cosmos. We are the products not only of our inner societies but also of the society we perceive. Yet we endure with a self-conscious identity, so that we know who we are, as we affect and have an effect on whatever is around us. We are chemical combinations that are not worth much, except within the structure of what we are becoming. The social system operating within us is not different from that operating in an animal, except that there is a tension between the bodily and mental poles which is different at our level of existence.

In this process of becoming and perishing, we move toward novelty. Life offers us the bid of freedom whereby we may build on what has perished as we become new creations. These novelties may be introduced for any reason or none, but when they are guided by purpose, ideals, and value they point to the major difference between human beings and other animals. Because we are constantly changing, there is no specific concrete identity, but running through the process our body remains generally identifiable and our awareness of ourselves as persons constitutes our self-consciousness. We grow as individuals in relationship, and we are constituted by the relationships we experience and affect. We do not control our environment, we are not creators, and ultimately we do not determine the world's destiny, but we do learn to align our aims with God's so that we respond to a love that is beyond us and experience the transforming power of God's grace.

At the center of our consciousness is the sense of worth. To be human, to exist at all, is to feel worthy. This confidence in our worth gives us the basis for moral action and for belief in God. We are enabled by recognition of the worth of others to trust, and ultimately to trust God as well as ourselves and others. When we lose this sense of worth and come to despise ourselves, we find that our ability to relate to others and to God vanishes.

During much of the twentieth century, we have been alternating between optimism and pessimism about the world's future. When there was a sense of economic security, a kind of confidence grew that was not based on the worth of human beings as such, and thus an economic slump led to pessimism. Catastrophes, wars, and moral scandals are always a threat to the optimistic hopes. Humanistic goals without religious resources are insufficient to keep alive the sense of worth in such times.

The sense of worth has always been supported by the Christian emphasis that men and women are made in the image of God. The psalmist wrote that we are "little lower than God." When we deal with each other, even in situations that reveal scandalous and immoral activity, we always look for some element of goodness, and we are upset when a person who is obviously guilty is unable to understand or confess guilt. The response of David to Nathan's charge that he was the guilty person is understandable, but if he had denied that taking Bathsheba had any moral implications we would have been dismayed.

There is a dualism in human nature that makes it possible to see human beings as the lowest of animals and as children of God. We belong to two kingdoms: the animal kingdom and the kingdom of God. The tensions of life are often those between these two kingdoms. There is no great difference between them, except in the goals that are served, for what is normal for an animal is frequently perversity in human beings. The difference between human and

121

nonhuman animals is first of all the existence of language, which results in a capacity to make finer moral distinctions, and at the highest level to be religious. There may be some elements of morality in animal behavior, but it is higher at the human level. Only human beings are formed by unrealized ideals that lead to novelty, and these purposes are derived from alignment with the purposes of God.

## THE ANIMAL KINGDOM

The human being is an animal and shares many capacities and functions with other animals. These animal functions are essential for survival. All animals kill. Big fish eat little ones, buzzards and goats eat almost anything, cats eat mice, and human beings eat members of the bovine species with particular relish. Rule Number One of the animal kingdom is *kill to eat.* All animals of carnivorous kinds do this, and there is no reason why they should not. Then there is Rule Number Two. All animals are competitive and this leads to conflict. When two dogs bark at each other, the barking becomes louder and hostility rises until something happens. Dogs are more prone to do this than other animals because, as Harry Emerson Fosdick suggested, "the dog is more nearly human." Rarely does this lead to killing, however, except in cases of some males who fight over females and vice versa—a question of sex. Rule Number Three carries us beyond the activity of dogs to a lower form of animal behavior. Hans Zinsser reminded us that only two species kill each other without provocation of hunger, self-defense, or sex: *rats and human beings.* There may be others, but this comparison makes the point. Even here there is a difference: Rats act by instinct and use their natural abilities. So Rule Number Four applies only to human beings. We use all the allies of our superior intelligences, imaginations, technical skills, and volitions to slaughter each other, although these gifts were given to us in order to align ourselves with God's purposes. Indeed, we even invoke God's blessing on our wanton killing. But human beings are superior to rats, because they improve on nature. Nuclear weapons, obliteration bombing, chemical warfare, and conscription of citizens are artificial from the point of view of the natural animal. God has given us freedom, and the result has been a constant succession of big and little, declared and undeclared wars which outdo the kingdom of rats in their savagery.

> I, a thin veneer on a soulless ball:
> Is that all?
> I, made in the image of God divine:
> Am I thine?
> I, evolved from the deep primeval slime:
> Is there time
> To seek thy kingdom before thy judgment falls
> On our sinful kind?
> O Lord, have mercy, have mercy upon us all!

There are other elements in the animal kingdom which human beings share and which are more desirable. There is creature-feeling, which culminates in group consciousness and in interpersonal relations, and ultimately in love. Even this, however, can be corrupted by false ideals. There are reproductive activities, which are raised to a new level because of the possibilities of choice and the association with love. The pleasures of the physical organism are those of the animal kingdom and have their own intrinsic values. Both dogs and human beings enjoy their walks together. Most of the conditions leading to good health are the same as in animals. *Human beings partake of the best and the worst of animal life, and go beyond the animals in both directions.*

There is a difference between human beings and animals. We are more complex beings, who have become self-critical, who can delay gratification in order to seek projected goals, who are at home in this world and yet wish to make it over into something better. In spite of the way in which we are determined by our en-

vironment, as animals are, we can be transformed while continuing our self-identity, and in the process of becoming and perishing
we can become new creatures bent on making a new world.
Because of this, we rise above the animal kingdom and enter into
the realm of value and obligation, of freedom and intelligence, and
of devotion to God. But the worst aspects of the animal kingdom,
of which we alone are subject, keep licking at our heels so that we
could easily destroy ourselves and the known world.

## What Human Beings Do

We do a number of things which differentiate us from other
animals. We might look at the following list: We laugh, talk, play
imaginatively, use tools and machines, reason, worship, rear
cultures, choose community, and suffer conflict usually of our own
making.[1] Our organisms, which are societies of functions or processes constantly becoming and perishing, respond to our environment in many different ways, some predictable and some not. We
have wills and minds, and we use freedom and intelligence in
meeting familiar and new situations. We are able to project courses
of action and to follow through on them. We are able to conceive
of values which ought to be achieved, and then to seek the means
whereby they may be brought to fruition.

In all of our functions, we know ourselves as intimately bound
up with the processes of nature, and yet we are able to stand apart
from nature. We are able to know, to judge, and to make decisions
as persons. We can choose between cooperating with the forces of
nature and finding means of controlling and exploiting nature. In
all of these activities, we know ourselves as persons, as unique individuals capable of a degree of solitariness and yet inevitably
related to other persons.

1. See Henry Nelson Wieman and Walter Marshall Horton, *The Growth
of Religion* (Chicago: Willett, Clark, 1938), pp. 449–479.

*Mind.* We have minds. By this we mean that we are conscious of events in the past, present, and future. We have memories of the past which are as real as experiences of the present, and we can use these memories of events which have perished as a basis for understanding the present and of choosing for the future. We are both conscious and self-conscious. We take the data of our experience and interpret them so that they have meaning for ourselves and others. We select the data we require in order to solve particular problems. A camera merely records what is there, but we can take the picture and see its beauty, make plans for war, or throw it away. Partly this is because we always approach the data from a particular perspective, but also because we can have an objectivity that a camera does not have.

As knowers, we are capable of judgment. We are able to relate seemingly unconnected facts in such a way that we bring new knowledge into existence. We can take experiences of value and judge between them. We can ignore some data because they do not fit into our way of viewing things. We can take our paycheck and use it for a night of carousing or for food for the family. There are many other things which we do, such as formulating gigantic systems of generalized concepts, making use of inventive genius to produce new machines, discovering new sources and uses of energy, seeing into the harmony of the spheres and composing great music, and rising to magnificent acts of heroism.

*Freedom.* We do not always do these things, for we belong to the animal kingdom and can use all the powers of the human mind to seek the lowest levels of animal behavior, or at least settle for a mixture between moral and immoral activity. We can make such choices, for presupposed in all that we have said is that we have freedom. Our minds would have little significance if they could be programmed or conditioned by environment and heredity. There is no doubt that the sphere of free thought and action is limited by external conditions, by the development of habits and a self-system, and that we tend to play it safe when our anxieties are high. But we can know when these limitations are affecting us and take steps to maintain our freedom within such limitations or take steps to break out of them—at a risk. Freedom implies both choice and responsibility. The law courts recognize that we are able to make free choices and can be held guilty for our actions, although they also recognize that conditions may apply that condone our selves if not our actions, so that there are, for example, distinctions between first- and second-degree murder, manslaughter, and not guilty by reason of insanity.

In order for there to be moral responsibility, we must have sufficient freedom to be a controlling factor in determining our own conduct. The latest discoveries in physics and psychology make room for indeterminacy, chance, and novelty, and thus for freedom. Charles Hartshorne wrote that "no events are completely determined or completely undetermined by their causes," and yet "all parts of nature are subject to habits, laws, causes."[2] If God works as the creativity in our midst, and if we can respond to God's aims as God's presence is manifest, we can expect novelty in our lives and in history, and we can respond in freedom to the lure of God's leading.

Our acts are determined by the strongest motive present, but *we determine which is the strongest motive!* We are not fully determined by it, because a motive is always sufficiently general to allow some means of choice. Habits may guide actions, but no matter how crystallized habits may become they never reach a stage of absoluteness. We are not likely to stop drinking, smoking, being sexually promiscuous, behaving greedily in business, misusing political power, or shortchanging our customers simply because we will it; but if the motivation is strong enough changes do take place. There is, then, a real freedom which is partial but effective in daily living, and which is the basis for genuine moral responsibility. In every moment of time, we are governed by our past acts, by our heredity, by our environment, and by a dominant motivation, but it is *a new moment, set off from the past, and just*

2. *Beyond Humanism* (Chicago: Willet, Clark, 1937), p. 150.

*as we know ourselves as distinct from other selves so we know this
act as distinct, a novel opportunity for choice and action.* Thus our
past perishes that we may become.

Christianity has always taught that we are free, that we are intelligent, and that we are self-conscious, as has the Greek tradition
in philosophy and most humanist ways of life, and occasionally
Christianity has been more guilty than others of blunting this truth,
especially through infelicitous statements about the sovereignty of
God and predestination.

The view of humanity proposed here is that we view each human
being as an "organism as a whole." The physical and mental poles
are so interrelated that it is impossible to consider one without the
other. Yet the mental is included within the physical, and a society
of cells working together leads to what it is to be a person. Christianity, as it comes to terms with medicine and psychiatry, sees
persons and their relations in an organismic manner, and thus the
ministry of pastors and physicians is to the whole person in relation
to other persons. The *will to belong* is essential to mental, spiritual,
and physical health. "To be human," wrote Daniel Day Williams,
"is to desire to belong, to have the security of being recognized in a
group which accepts us, speaks our language, holds our values,
gives us our freedom to move as we will."[3] This becomes possible in
the family, and in other groups such as clubs, schools, and churches, but when it goes wrong it ends in self-deification as we seek
to protect our way of life against any other, or it leads to anxiety
over not belonging, a kind of ostracism that is unbearable. Because
of our racial, ethnic, social class, and sexual differences, the need to
belong is threatened for many people, and we need to see how God
fits into the picture.

## CHILDREN OF GOD

We are different from other animals because we are worshippers
of God, who, in turn, places a special value on us. We have a sense

3. *The Spirit and Forms of Love* (New York: Harper & Row, 1968), p.
147.

of worth, of belonging to a society that is more human than anything else, of having a destiny in relation to God. If God works through the processes which create value and sustain us in our spiritual quests, our achievement of selfhood is intimately connected with the working of God in the world.

Jesus, as recorded in the synoptic Gospels, held a higher view of humanity than did his contemporaries or his followers, as for example, Paul's view in the early chapters of the letter to the Romans, where persons are seen as almost hopeless, predestined to their end, and saved only by God's merciful transaction on the cross. It is said that Paul's doctrine of God's grace is more inclusive than that of Jesus. This is because Paul's view is that we are helpless and in need of help from the beginning, while Jesus teaches that we have a sense of worth and a freedom to choose as a basis for experiencing God's grace. The image of God in humanity is not nearly as badly defaced in Jesus' thought as in Paul's. God has endowed us with sufficient spiritual power to make our own decisions. We may still choose to live among swine and yet we have not lost the power to "come to ourselves." *We can turn, and that is the basis for hope.* As a matter of empirical fact, we can observe those who are transformed and are able to find in God's supportive grace the power and direction to align themselves with God's aims.

*Sin.* Sin is disloyalty to God, a missing of the mark, a failure to align our aims with those of God as we understand them. The image of God in humanity is defaced, but it is this image that makes us decision-making persons. The image of God is conceived in terms of love, so that the basis for sin is the failure to love, or it may be a perverted or impotent form of love. It is very much like a disease that takes away from us our power to think and will what is right. It leaves us with a distorted sense of God, who becomes an enemy, and therefore we are unable to trust God.

The sources of sin in us may be traced to a variety of experiences. Traditionally the emphasis has been on an exaggerated self-love, which leads to self-aggrandisement at the expense of others. The sense of worth, which is essential for moral and mental health, gets out of control so that we see others as of less worth. Sin also arises from interpersonal anxiety, so that in our insecurity we develop a self-system that is primarily protective against the uncanny dread of relating to others. This leads to alienation from others and from God and finally to ostracism as a fact of experience.[4] This is closely related to the feeling of despising one's own self, and therefore to the self-fulfilling activity based on disparagement of what is worthwhile. Thus the sinner can identify one's self as "a worm" in God's sight.

The word *sin* points to a human condition but also to less than human actions by individuals and groups and nations. Yet human beings, as well as groups and nations, can transcend the sinful aspects of human nature. This is what the Gospel is all about. The glory of humanity at its highest is that we have the potentiality to be "but little lower than God." We do not control God, we do not control the future, we do not control other human beings, we do not control nature. Human beings are made in the *image* of God, but we must never for a moment think that the image *is* God.

We forget that God is the creative order and that we are God's creatures. The psalmist does not forget, for after stating the high position granted to human beings, he concludes with "O Lord, Our Governor, how glorious is thy name in all the earth!" But we are not content to rest in a subordinate position. As in the story of the tower of Babel, we think that we can go beyond the limits placed upon us and become as God. We seek power over other persons, to put them in subjection to us rather than to God. We are pleased with our power and associate it with goodness, forgetting how power can corrupt us. Thus we suffer from the sin of pride.

Our sin is not that we are limited, for we are limited by our finite status, but in our refusal to accept that limitation. Sometimes, of course, we are so satisfied with our lower status that we remain on

4. See Harry Stack Sullivan, *Theory of Interpersonal Psychiatry* (New York: Norton, 1953).

the animal level and thus fail to fulfill the meaning of what it is to be human or humane. So we let loose all the passions of the animal kingdom, supplement them with the instruments God gave us to rise above the animal kingdom, and thus sink below the animal kingdom. Our worst sins consist of combining the lust for power with animal lust, ending in complete rebellion against God. This, in turn, arouses God's judgment, and persons, nations, and even civilizations are destroyed.[5]

Jesus made a distinction between two kinds of people: (1) the person who prays, "I thank God I am not as other men," and in so doing betrays one's pride as the essential sinfulness; (2) the sinner who prays, "Lord, have mercy on me, a sinner." But there are many ways in which these attitudes may be shaded toward each other. A person may be inconsistent in loyalty, so that there is variety in one's behavior; one may substitute loyalty to some bad or good cause for commitment to God; one may refuse to see or act out the implications of this loyalty; one may prefer loyalty to a lesser value, such as business, country, family, or almost any human endeavor; one may even take pride in the sin that makes grace abound.

Human beings are complex, and no analysis can be complete, but certainly Shakespeare was close to the mark when he wrote in *Measure for Measure:*

> . . . but man, proud man!
> Dress'd in a little brief authority, —
> Most ignorant of what he's most assured,
> His glassy essence, —like an angry ape,
> Plays such fantastic tricks before high heaven
> As make the angels weep. . . .

*The Process of Salvation.* Jesus told the story of salvation in the parable of the prodigal son. There is always danger of trying to get

---

5. See Reinhold Niebuhr, *The Nature and Destiny of Man*, Vol. I (New York: Scribners, 1941), pp. 178 ff.

more than one lesson out of a parable, but this drama does not break down. A man had two sons, and both of them shared in the father's inheritance. There was no difference in their worth in their father's eyes. The younger son by his own choice went to a far country. He spent his inheritance and lived a riotous life. In time he was in despair and want. At last, he came to himself and realized that this was not the life for him. However unhappy he had been at home, he was less happy here. Being free from all restraints did not turn out to be fun after all. He yearned to be home. He knew himself for what he was. And he said, "I will arise and go to my father." The son had the courage and the freedom to decide and act. He would place himself in his father's hands. He was willing to accept a position as servant or slave, for he knew he was unworthy. But his father was looking for him, and ran out to greet him, not stopping to listen to his prepared speech. The reception was joyous. There was no hedging in the son's return. This was no New Year's resolution. The son was humble, contrite, and ready to do his father's bidding. The father received him unconditionally. He was not received as a guest or servant or slave, but was reinstated as a son. The son, who was dead in his father's eyes, had come to life. The father rejoiced because the son had been found again. Although we must not allegorize a parable, we can say that the process was like that of salvation, in that the son was delivered from his alienation and was restored to the community of his own home. The main note is the joy of the father and the celebration following the son's return. But the parable is not ended, for it deals with *two lost sons.* The elder son was probably a good boy who stayed at home, went to the synagogue on the Sabbath, and did whatever his father commanded. Was not his complaint justified? "All these years," he whined, "I have been slaving for you." There was lack of understanding here. He could not understand his father's joy at the return of his brother. He referred to his brother as *"your* son," "this son of *yours."* Here we have the man of pride who thanks God that he is not as other men are. He did his duty simply because it was his duty, with a purely mercenary attitude.

131

He was good in a negative and colorless sort of way. He was a *second lost son.* He could not open his heart, which was constricted with harsh and bitter feelings.

We need not identify the father with God to get the point of the parable. The key question is, "What do you think?" The focus at the end is on the loving father. We are not to praise or condemn either son, but we should seek to understand them. The story is a warning of how ethics is barren without religion, of how so-called good people can be the worst sinners, and of how the sin of those who go through the motions of religion, who love beauty and forms and ceremonial, can prevent them from opening their essential being to the processes of reconciliation for themselves or others. It is not advice to emulate the younger son with riotous living, either. It does tell us how a loving parent responds to either type of child. As a parable, it helps us think about parents and children, as well as about God and ourselves.[6]

The parables about lost sons, lost sheep, and lost coin point to a single theme: The lost will be found, the dead will come to life, the alienated will be restored to fellowship. The agents are respectively a father, a shepherd, and a woman. They are not necessarily models for God, but they serve an analogical purpose. The choice of a woman in the parable of the lost coin is important for a number of reasons: It points to the significance of women in Jesus' thinking, it reminds us of the importance of women in the early church, and it indicates that the feminine aspects of life can be used analogically when speaking of God. Again, the challenge is, "What do you think?"

*Human Destiny.* If we start with the individual's sense of worth for an understanding of humanity, we are faced with a major problem. It is similar to the claim that all of us are created free and equal. It is obvious, in the light of history, that there are great

---

6. See Charles W. F. Smith, *The Jesus of the Parables* (Philadelphia: Pilgrim Press, 1975), pp. 74–80.

varieties of equality within groups and between groups. If in Christ there is neither male nor female, black nor white, peon nor landlord, it becomes obvious that Christ does not have much to do with things as they are. If the church represents Christ and we look at the ways in which the church has treated minorities, we cannot have much hope about the future.

The claim we make as Christians is clear enough. One's race or sex or social class makes no difference in our worth. We have the right to use whatever gifts God has given us to serve others as Christians. This should mean that no handicaps are placed before any person on account of race or sex or social class. It does not mean that real differences are obliterated. There are biological and sexual functions that are part of the givenness of life. There are probably some advantages biologically in terms of size, color, and other aspects of human development.

How these problems should be worked out in terms of liberation, of freedom from oppression, of economic opportunity, or even of ministry in the church is not immediately clear, for there are many voices. What needs to be recognized is that there needs to be a reexamination of roles at all levels, for if we are to be more human than we are racial or sexual, we need to look even more carefully at what it means to be human. The knocking down of barriers is a cooperative task arising out of dialogue and mutual understanding, with the dominant factor being the desire that the other be liberated. It is entirely possible that the dominant white male is as imprisoned by his role as the white female is restricted by childrearing duties at home. Whites are facing barriers when they seek dialogue with blacks, although blacks have faced greater barriers for longer times.

The church has a poor record. Dominated by white male theologians and often by celebate male leaders, women have been given little place as persons, although they have served loyally in the place given to them. But are we waiting for the possibility that a pope might miss Easter mass because *she* is at home in Kenya having a baby? This would only be a symbol, like Queen Elizabeth

II in England, but as it could only happen if women had equal treatment throughout the hierarchy it may have some significance as a hope.

Behind these comments is the recognition of the sense of worth at the center of the Gospel. With this valuing of the person, fulfillment should be possible at any level simply due to the fact of being human, rather than in terms of race, sex, or social class. Because human beings also differ in terms of potential, the opportunities for service would be in terms of the gifts we have received, not ones we do not have. But this is as it should be.

We have real freedom, and we can accept or reject the rich possibilities of a life committed to the will of God. No person can fully escape *confrontation* with God, although one may avoid using the concept, and the choice is between commitment and judgment. These are the two extremes, but no one ever reaches completely either one. The atheist unconsciously does good in cooperation with the creative and redemptive order of reality which others call God, but the atheist is *not consciously* committed and therefore lacks some of the intellectual and conceptual values. A person who accepts *belief* in God as a formal creed and then fails to live in commitment to God is not likely to enter the kingdom. There are all degrees of religious living, and most of us are somewhere in the middle, doing good and evil, consciously and unconsciously.

Jesus asked his followers to turn and follow him in his commitment to God. Individuals who are consciously committed to God and God's work in the world recognize their shortcomings, which are present in spite of their good intentions, and they are able to keep sane views in spite of suffering; they have resources for living which enable them to find essential values in all places; and they are integrated because their trust in God points toward God's processes in the world. The abundant life leads to better health, the ability to endure suffering and to transcend it, less tension and anguish, greater appreciation of the goods of this life no matter what one's economic status may be, and a willingness to serve others. Thus one becomes concerned about the misery and suffering of others, the loss of freedom in many nations, and the acts one can take to achieve a more just social order. There are serenity mixed with humility, relaxation combined with effective activity, joyousness blended with a sense of tragedy in such a life. Those who are fully committed to God become mature in the human meaning of that term. The use of a creative mind and will, backed by the resources of prayer and worship, does much for individuals and for society.

Human destiny involves the facing of death. Jesus taught us how to live and how to die. There are rapidly changing attitudes toward death and an afterlife. The widespread practice of cremation indicates less emphasis on the physical body. But is there any basis for belief in life after death? Obviously, this is not an area where we can be guided by experience. Yet immortality is considered a reasonable hope by many people. If God is good and human persons have value in God's sight, if God is the conserver of values and we have value, then it is reasonable to suppose that God will provide for some continuance of human personality. We cannot prove this, but neither can we disprove it. It is for many a corollary to the Christian belief about God and human beings. It accounts for some of the undeserved evils of this world, for infant death, for unrealized potentialities in the development of persons, and for the conservation of human values.

There is another approach to immortality which commends itself to some people. If God is understood as the one who prehends all that we think and do, if in God's memory our own values are transformed, if God as suffering love shares our joy and sorrows, positively prehends what is good, transforms what is evil, and negatively prehends or rejects what cannot serve as a basis for future good, we can begin to understand that there is what Whitehead called "objective" immortality. We as subjects do not experience "subjective" immortality in that our personalities do not endure as self-conscious "souls," but what we stand for endures everlastingly and "objectively" in God.

There was a time when George Washington did not exist, but now that he has existed there will never be a time when we can say he did not exist. Charles Hartshorne puts the theory this way:

> There was once no such individual as myself, even as something that was "going to exist." But centuries after my death, there will have been that very individual which I am. This is creation, with no corresponding decreation. But, again, what then is death?

Death is the last page of the last chapter of the book of one's life, as birth is the first page of the first chapter. Without a first page there is no book. But given the first page there is, so far, a book. The question of death then is, How rich and how complete is the book to be?[7]

For this book to have value, there must be a reader, and for some generations after we die our book can be read by our successors. But in time they will cease to be. Even now, they will be unable to grasp the whole book. But, according to Hartshorne, God reads our book everlastingly. God omits nothing and adds nothing. So there is an important way in which we continue to live in God's memory. This belief conforms to what we know empirically about life and death, and for those of us who think of God in this way such a concept of "objective" immortality is satisfying.[8]

Christianity offers us the abundant life. If we live life to the full, finding our destiny in the love of God and in our love for others, there will be values for us past all understanding. Amidst all the tragedy of the world, there will be a foundation which will stand in the face of suffering, death, and the collapse of Western culture. The Christian religion is realistic in that it faces these things rather than escapes from them. There is no real hope or faith in the ostrich type of religion which evades moral, spiritual, and social issues.

7. Charles Hartshorne, *The Logic of Perfection and Other Essays* (LaSalle, Illinois: Open Court Publishing Co., 1962), pp. 250–251.
8. See my *Live Until You Die* (Philadelphia: United Church Press, 1973), pp. 126–129.

There is an assurance that, when we live out our Christian faith to the full, we will be in a right relationship with God and other persons. If there are abiding values in the achievements of this present time, and if there is everlasting significance in the commitment of ourselves to God, then life is worth living whether there be subjective immortality or not; and we may let life after death take care of itself as a possibility. Our destiny is to live and die in complete devotion to the God revealed through Jesus Christ, and if there be any heavenly reward we can safely leave the time and place in the hands of God. And if this life is all there is, that does not contradict our basic faith, for we believe that God prehends us and what we have to offer in our thoughts and actions—and that is enough, for God is everlasting.

# 9
# *Does Prayer Work?*

Christianity is a religion of strength. It does not lead to physical power directly, but it provides a sustaining strength for the total person in the face of obstacles. The great saints of the church and their little bands of followers have had access to this power. Albert Schweitzer, Thomas Merton, Madeleine Barot, Martin Luther King, Dietrich Bonhoffer, and Sister Teresa are names to be reckoned with in modern Christianity because in them and their followers we see something of the heroic stature of religious faith. They simply have resources which most of us do not have. They turn to God and the power comes. In every case of great spiritual achievement, there is at the heart of it a life of devotion. Dag Hammarskjöld's *Markings* gives us a record of what one committed civil servant thought about. The prayers of such people are varied and the techniques differ, but each of them is able to be open to the subjective aims of God and to align the individual to the cosmic purpose.

Prayer is primarily an attitude toward God. It is a response to the lure of feeling, a feeling that God is with us and that we are in the heart of God. It is an awesome presence, so that we do not reduce this attitude to one of selfish desires expressed in miscellaneous, pious, and platitudinous words. When we pray, an attitude is created which leads to spiritual power, a power which changes our personalities by guiding, encouraging, reconditioning, and con-

138

verting our innermost selves, so that we may offer ourselves for the
service of God.

The problem of one who prays may be compared to that of a
pearl diver. The diver has fulfilled all the conditions before seeking
the pearl. Having trained the body, knowing where to dive, desir-
ing the pearl with urgency, and committing one's self to the deep,
in the words of Browning:

> Are there not—
> Two points in the adventure of the diver:
> One—when a beggar, he proposes to plunge,
> One—when a prince, he rises with his pearl?

We also prepare ourselves for prayer, and then commit ourselves to
the deep of God's spiritual reservoir, and the pearl is the power to
do God's will.

The purpose and effect of prayer are not to change God's will.
Prayer changes us! Prayer has been misunderstood by those who
claim that God can be coerced, or that prayer is *only* autosuggestion, or that prayer will change the conditions around us.
Because prayer has been interpreted as magic, as fooling ourselves,
and as a shortcut for accepting social responsibilities, it has been
discredited by the less discerning.

Prayer is not magic. Religion in its primitive form was closely
allied with magic, so that Plato called religion "the science of beg-
ging and getting from the gods." This is a debased form of religion,
where the emphasis is on *my* will. God is cajoled, bribed, and per-
suaded to water *my* crops, to make *our* armies safe, to eliminate
*my* particular troubles. There are people who make bargains with
God: "Give me a new automobile and I will go to church for a
whole year." If the automobile arrives, the bargain is usually
forgotten. It might be proper to pray for a new car, but not in terms
of bribery and then failing to keep the bargain.

Prayer is related to autosuggestion. Certainly when we plant ideas in our minds in terms of goals to be realized and then reassert these goals in terms of prayer, this is a form of autosuggestion, but there is a sense in which this stimulates one's larger and better self, so that one is enabled to achieve the goal. This may be one of the least significant of the ways of prayer. It is subjective, and may only touch on the reality of God tangentially. But if it results in some kind of moral growth, we may believe that God is at work.

Prayer is not a substitute for works. One cannot expect a concrete result from prayer unless proper conditions are fulfilled. There is no "Let God do it" attitude about genuine prayer. Prayer becomes a means for letting loose those energies which are necessary for the obtaining of desired results, but unless these energies are directed by persons the results will not come to pass. It is legitimate to pray for better race relations, slum clearance, or the overcoming of hunger, but unless the human and social conditions are fulfilled which make those processes possible there can be no answer to prayer.

Prayer leads to action, and in the effect of prayer we see its objective validity. Prayer may lead to unexpected and seemingly miraculous results through natural channels. Prayer "is already incipient action."[1] It is the center of religious behavior, because in prayer there is a relationship between God and us as human organisms are opened to the impact of the creative processes toward value in the world and we make a commitment to what we perceive to be God's aim for us.

Prayer is a means of focusing on God's presence. There is a disclosure of God's ingression into our lives, a discernment that the God who is everywhere is also here with us. By means of words, symbols, ikons, and models of thinking, we are enabled to focus on the presence which stands behind and is never identical with the means. Sometimes we need words and at other times we are reduced to silence.

1. T. H. Green, *Works*, III (New York: Kraus Reprint, 1968), p. 274.

God himself is with us;
Let us all adore him,
And with awe appear before him.
God is here within us;
Soul, in silence fear him,
Humbly, fervently draw near him.
Now his own
Who have known
God, in worship lowly,
Yield their spirits wholly.[2]

## HOW PRAYER FUNCTIONS

It is hard to know exactly what prayer does. So many claims are made for its efficiency that seem to be mere coincidence, especially in terms of specific results, that many of us remain skeptical. When two people "get guidance" not to go on a certain plane, and that plane crashes and kills most of the passengers, it can hardly be conceived as an answer to prayer, for if God is a loving God who controls plane crashes there would be no accidents. We cannot conceive of God's working in this way. However, if the pilot, because of a sensitive and appreciative response to a dangerous situation, succeeds in making a safe landing, there might be some claim that this awareness is a form of response to God's aim for him. It is a natural channel of God's activity.

It is possible to "prehend" God in the context of a problem, so that we bring to the problem indirectly whatever awareness we have of God's aim for us. This is different from the desperate approach of seeking God when other avenues of decision and action are blocked; it is not a God-of-last-resort approach. Rather, it is a bringing of our awareness of God's presence and aim into the

2. Gerhardt Tersteegen (1729), from *The Hymnal 1940*, No. 477 (New York: Church Hymnal Corp., 1943).

decision-making process. One can speak of being "grounded" in God. A radio without a ground wire suffers from static, uneven reception, and outside interference. This model suggests that a person not grounded in God is thrown off balance by unexpected suffering, by waves of opinion that contradict one's ideals and values, and pressures both internal and external that lead to deviation from God's aims. Prayer, by grounding us in God, provides steadfastness, stability, and direction. It cleanses and purifies, so that the obstacles to the processes of spiritual growth are removed.

The habit of prayer is a corrective to other habits. Although habits are essential to human living and provide a structure for the self-system, habits which are crystallized eliminate the possibility of entering into experiences of greater riches. One of the most important habits is developing new habits, and prayer keeps open the channels of appreciation so that growth of habits may take place. Because God is the source of new values, our capacity to bring our higher potentialities into the realm of the actual is made more effective through prayer.

Prayer is a source of strength for facing all obstacles. The confused, discouraged, or defeated person may through prayer find those resources which make it possible to overcome many difficulties. The courage to face an operation, the strength to confess a wrong done to a friend, the ability to eliminate traits which make one a wallflower, the incentive to try a new adventure in business, or the stimulus to face various kinds of injustice and oppression may come from the sense of power that emanates from communion with God. If God is the source of all values, and if processes of creativity bring such values into actuality, our task is, so to speak, to get on board and ride those processes to their destination. Prayer is a means for becoming a cooperative agency with those processes and a servant of God.

Prayer is a source of comfort in the face of inevitable events. The person who faces certain death with equanimity, the family which rises in the circumstances of destitution and adjusts to unavoidable poverty, the crippled individual who continues to do those things which are still possible and finds new ways of doing the unexpected, and the parents who have to place a handicapped child in an institution can find the resources which make their lot bearable and honorable through prayer.

Prayer is a means of insight. In the act of prayer we become susceptible to stimuli which are absent from the habitual responses to environment. Through the gleaning of new data, we may reach different perspectives, new concepts, or new directions of action. We are changed through prayer. We see the wickedness or uselessness of our previous ways and resolve to turn from our wickedness and live. We find new data which give us new interpretations of the meaning of God for human living. These things occur because the conditions of prayer, the quiet, the relaxation, and the open awareness that accompany it, are different from the conditions of normal perception.

Prayer should always be in the spirit of *"Thy* will be done." Yet, it is right that we make petitions to God. In the purifying aspect of prayer, we confess our sins and express our repentance, we give thanks for God's goodness and love, we commit ourselves to God's will, and we express our own dominant desires in the light of God's will for us. We pray for that which is "most expedient for us." We pray for others in the same way. But when we pray for the fulfillment of our own desires or for welfare of others, we must meet the conditions if our prayers are to be answered. Prayer can lead to better health, the right use of money, the overcoming of bad habits, and fellowship with others, provided we meet the conditions. But prayer is always in terms of God's will, and therefore many prayers seem to be unanswered. One cannot forget the story of the old man who got up in prayer meeting and said, "I thank God that he has seen fit to say no to so many of my prayers."

What should we pray for? We should pray for whatever will make for the growth of value in the world. Christians pray in Jesus' name. One test would be, can you pray for that and end up with "for Jesus Christ's sake" as a criterion? Yet, as George Macdonald wrote, "Anything large enough for a wish to light upon, is large enough to hang a prayer upon: the thought of him to whom that prayer goes will purify and correct the desire."[3] Prayer is *affirmative* even when it is petitionary. Prayer is always the affirmation of God's aim in relation to our aims; it is an affirmation of *reality*.

The variety of prayer is clear to anyone who peruses a few devotional manuals. There is the one extreme where communion with God is found consciously only by retreating from the normal activities and responsibilities of life, regaining energy, and then taking part in the normal tasks of life again. In the race of life, it might be likened to the technique of the hare against the tortoise, for the hare must rest occasionally and then proceed with great rapidity. The other extreme is the technique of the tortoise, which always has one foot on the ground and keeps steadily at the task. An even better example might be the caterpillar which always has a number of legs on the ground while others are not. William James called the latter the tough-minded in contrast to the tender-minded. Both psychological types have their distinctive approaches to prayer and religious living.

Prayer does not necessarily require language but usually it does. Ian T. Ramsey suggests that (1) "its introductory language must lead us into God's presence and be logically suited to and adequate to that task. This means in particular that the personal words it contains will be suitably qualified." (2) "The phrases of the prayer must be consistent with our doctrine of God," avoiding the slot machine or the many-words approach. (3) "The prayer must name a situation or some state of affairs which can, in principle, be a focus of God's activity, whether as directed to ourselves, or influencing in some way the circumstances we have named, or both."[4]

The only way to develop a life of communion with God is to experiment. Words, postures, places, and other aids may be used,

3. *George Macdonald: An Anthology*, ed. C. S. Lewis (New York. Dolphin Books, 1962), No. 94, pp. 66–67.

4. Ian T. Ramsey, *Models for Divine Activity* (London: SCM, 1973), pp. 38–39.

but the fundamental thing is to find those ways by which our attitudes can point beyond ourselves to God. It is not a matter of techniques, although they may help. The most untraditional approach, which seems nonreligious to others, may suit you best. You may prefer wordless adoration, or simple reflection on the activities of the day, or cooperative planning in the face of a decision, or a relaxed form of openness in which there is no focus of attention at all. All you can do is try what seems acceptable and comfortable as ways of approaching God. It is not always easy, and sometimes God seems more like an enemy or a void than a friend.

We dare not say what prayer cannot do, and yet we need to be careful in claiming for prayer that which is mere coincidence or luck or accident. The evidence is hard to come by, for the effect of prayer is often indirect and tenuous, and something started at a distance in time and space may in due time affect the local situation. There is no test tube for prayer, but in the crucible of experience everywhere prayer has been the means of making human allies of God on God's grounds, and this has meant lives overflowing with the richness of goodness, and beauty and truth.

## CORPORATE WORSHIP

Private prayer is essential to religious living, but in itself is radically incomplete. Just as a person cannot live a Christian life without fellowship, so the prayer life of the Christian is supplemented by corporate worship. Like-minded Christians, sharing a common ethos, worship together by confessing their sins, becoming conscious of God's forgiveness, praising God for the benefits that come from the transforming and creative processes that the word God stands for, expressing their fundamental needs, making their petitions and intercessions, and listening to the Word of God in Scripture and sermon—this is the process of worship, whether it be found in a simple meeting house or in the ornate splendor of a high liturgy.

"Worship," says Bernard E. Meland, "is the *lunge toward reality.*

145

It is the conscious effort to throw off the sham, the superficial, the trivial and sordid crustations that gather about us in daily associations. Without this effort we tend to become calloused by social niceties and poses which, perhaps, are necessary concessions to the folkways of our environs, but invariably pernicious when not countered by a shrug of the shoulders or a vigorous effort to stand upright and attentive before standards and values that are objective and actual and before which we dare make no concessions."[5] Worship does for society what private prayer does for the individual, but because of the welding force of fellowship it does this with greater efficiency and on a greater scale. The natural effect of all religious living is deeper fellowship, and thus the act of corporate worship is in itself a symbol of the meaning of worship.

A group of worshippers gathers strength from their common sharing or prehending of God in relationship to themselves. As a prerequisite, this demands some common ground of belief and common use of religious language. Many of us have had the experience of worshipping, or of attempting to worship, where the theological assumptions and the language have become barriers. Especially important is a common belief about God's activity, a recognition of God's nature as other than ourselves and yet as operating within a common view of the universe and what happens within it.

What is held in common is an intuition that at the center of life there is a God who loves and therefore shares our suffering, who acts to transform us and to restore us to spiritual wholeness, and to whom we offer our commitment and thanksgiving. This leads to an attitude of adoration, and thus to greater sensitivity to God's presence, resulting in a deeper moral commitment to those values which make life worthwhile. God is sought not for the sake of our human destiny but for God's sake alone.

If worship is a "lunge toward reality," and if we are attracted by

---

5. Bernard E. Meland, *Modern Man's Worship* (New York: Harper & Row, 1934), p. 228.

the lure of a more than human power, it follows that the instigator of worship is God. God's love is prior to human love. God's hands are held out to us before we reach for them. As Evelyn Undershill wrote, "the easy talk of the pious naturalist," of a human "approach to God is both irrational—indeed plainly impudent—and irreverent; unless the priority of God's approach" to us "be kept in mind."[6] Worship is the recognition of human finitude, of human creatureliness, of the separation from God that needs healing; and the human response is a free act of devotion.

Worship, to use a different set of metaphors, is the *vertical* relationship between God and human beings that makes possible the *horizontal* relationship between persons. God's love is the source of human fellowship. The two commands, to love God and to love others, are *equal,* but the priority of God's love is everlasting. This is recognized by those who come together to express their common affirmations, aspirations, and failings. Worship at its best is the cement that holds the bricks of the world together. It is the means for getting at the *source* of our values. Without God, human beings do not achieve their full humanity; and without worship, human beings do not come into relationship with God.

The worshipping community holds itself together because of its common memory. It recites the story whereby the church came into existence, and by centering on the work of Jesus Christ it recalls the reconciling work of God in history and our hope for the future. Memory and hope are held together by means of worship. Its memory of the baptism of Jesus by John is related to its hope for the future of all people through the sacrament of baptism. The Holy Communion is a memorial of a specific event in the life of Jesus, but it is also a celebration of God's current activity in the world. The recalling of Jesus' death and resurrection becomes the motif of those who are lost and found, are dead and alive again, in today's world. "The suffering, atoning, and redeeming love of God is remembered

6. Evelyn Underhill, *Worship* (New York: Harper & Row, 1937), p. 7.

and represented ever anew when the sacrament is celebrated, and, we most certainly add, when it is received in faith."[7]

There is a vision shared by people in a congregation, and this "vision claims nothing but worship. . . . That religion is strong which in its ritual and its mode of thought evokes an apprehension of the commanding vision. The worship of God is not a rule of safety—it is an adventure of the spirit, a flight after the unattainable. The death of religion comes with the repression of the high hope of adventure."[8] When God is placed outside the processes by which we live and becomes an absentee deity, when we worship by playing safe and avoiding the radical aims of God, when we stay within the law of tradition and lose its spirit, then our worship is but a joyless duty. But when God is our everlasting companion, when every act of worship is an adventure, when our memory of the tradition is combined with our hope for the future, then our worship is "an apprehension of the commanding vision."

## THE LORD'S PRAYER

The model for Christian prayer is the Lord's Prayer. It is no liturgical formula, no long-drawn-out device to bring about the satisfaction of our petty needs. It can be said reverently in thirty seconds, and one could meditate on each phrase for many hours. It has been called "a series of perfect desires," and it includes every prayerful attitude. It is the epitome of our seeking after God.

> Seek the LORD while he may be found,
> Call upon him while he is near!
> Let the wicked forsake his way,
> And the unrighteous man his thoughts;
> And let him return to the LORD, that he may have pity on him,
> And to our God, for he shall abundantly pardon (Is. 55:6–7,G).

7. Daniel Day Williams, *The Spirit and Forms of Love* (New York: Harper & Row, 1968), p. 190.

8. Alfred North Whitehead, *Science and the Modern World* (New York: Macmillan, 1925), pp. 268–269.

Boynton Merrill has likened the prayer to a giant bird. It begins and ends on the wings of praise, carrying us toward God. In the middle portion is the body, our fundamental needs and attitudes which are being carried on the wings of adoration and love.

"Pray then like this: Our Father who (or which) art in heaven, Hallowed be thy name." It is *our* Father whom we are addressing, not *my* Father or *your* Father. We are addressing the one whom we think of as the Father of humankind, who transcends our finite limitations, and yet who is accessible. Jesus used the word, *abba,* which is probably closer to "Daddy" than "Father" in today's world, thus stressing the significance of the closeness of the relationship.

But we add "hallowed," "holy," "revered" "be thy name." God has a name, Yahweh (YHWH), and it is so holy that it is not to be pronounced. It is a name that causes us to respond with awe and wonder. God is everywhere, and we cannot escape the divine presence. "If I climb up into heaven, thou art there; if I go down to hell, thou art there also" (Ps. 139:7,PB). "Yea, though I walk through the valley of the shadow of death, I will fear no evil; for thou art with me; thy rod and thy staff comfort me" (Ps. 23:4,PB). Here is the recognition of the numinous, the mysterious holiness of God which we only dimly fathom but enough so that we respond with reverence and a desire not to profane that name.

Then we ask for the coming of God's rule. "Thy kingdom come: Thy will be done on earth as it is in heaven." This is not submission; it is the affirmation that God's aims are to be accomplished in the here and now. May we so cooperate with God's purposes that God's sovereignty will be acknowledged by all. The metaphor that is used pictures a locale where God's purposes are working, in "heaven." We are seeking no earthly treasures, but only that we and all humankind may "do justly, love kindness, and walk humbly" with God. This urge for the coming of the kingdom, which is primarily an ethical thrust, outranks every other thought, because it is at the heart Christian discipleship. "It is not every one who says to me 'Lord, Lord!' who will get into the kingdom of heaven, but only those who do the will of my Father in heaven"

(Mt. 7:21,G). Our calling is to duplicate on earth the will which already rules in heaven, and this can be done through the processes of personal and social transformation.

There is recognition here of the work that may be done by well-meaning persons who are unconscious of being its agents. Archbishop Donald Coggan suggests that many scientists and politicians who may acknowledge no allegiance to the Christian faith are still able to further God's aims for people and nations, especially as they make possible those steps that need to be taken to achieve a more peaceful society, a society in which the goods of the earth are more equally shared, and a society in which truth is more nearly understood. "Wherever the forces of darkness, disease, and hate are driven back, there the kingdom comes, and God enters in more fully to the sovereignty of [God's] world."[9]

The phrase also points to the future with hope, for when the kingdom comes, when God's aims are fully achieved, then there will be rejoicing, for God's relationships with all creatures will remain unbroken. This is a utopian and eschatological goal, but it is still a proper topic for prayer.

"Give us this day our daily bread." The first specific request is for bread. It is hard, someone has said, to make love or to be religious on an empty stomach. Jesus saw more deeply than that; he saw that every person has the right to live. It is not give *me*; it is give *us* bread sufficient for the day. Even those who are well endowed with food must pray that all people might have their due. When Jesus said, "Feed my sheep," he might have meant it literally. We must remember that in the primitive church the duty of the deacons was to seek out the widows and orphans and to offer them food and shelter. The situation today is much more complex, and an attack on the food problem without attention to the population explosion, to economic privation among the less privileged nations, and to the suffering of those oppressed for political and economic reasons is a

9. Donald Coggan, *The Prayers of the New Testament* (New York: Harper & Row, 1967), p. 25.

simplification of the meaning of this petition. Every one of us ought to feel the shame and sin of it if we have not done all in our power to make it possible for all people to share God's generous gifts of the harvest. Walter Rauschenbusch observed that it was difficult for the malnourished and deprived even to hear the Gospel, much less respond to its good news. We need to remember always that God is the Lord of the fruits of the soil just as much as being Lord of history.

As the body of the prayer grows between the wings of praise, we come to the expression of humility and repentance: "Forgive us our trespasses." With repentance, however, is combined the sense of forgiveness tempered with supreme justice: "As we forgive those who trespass against us." We can ask God to treat us as we have treated our debtors. It is not a question of making a deal with God provided that we forgive others. It is rather an insight that unless we forgive others we are surely not to be forgiven. It can be combined with Jesus' statement, "Father, forgive them, for they know not what they do." Unless we can eradicate the hate that we have for others, however, we are going to have trouble with forgiveness, both for ourselves and for others, for vindictive people have difficulty with any prayer. Only penitent people can ask for forgiveness. "If thou, O Lord, shouldst record iniquities, O Lord, who could stand? But with thee there is forgiveness" (Psm, 130:3, G). Archbishop Coggan writes that beneath the two charred beams that make the cross in the ruins of Coventry Cathedral are two words, "Father, forgive." Not three words, not forgive *them*.[10] It is the nature of suffering love at the center of God's creativity to forgive. Therefore there is hope that we may be forgiven and restored to fellowship with God.

There are powers of evil in the world. Jesus may have believed in a personal devil, and the prayer can read, "Lead us not into temptation, but deliver us from the evil *one*." But first, we have trouble with the idea that God might lead us into temptation. It has been

10. Ibid., pp. 34–35.

151

variously translated: "Do not bring us to the test," "Let us not be put to the test," "Keep us from losing our faith in you," "Save us in the time of trial." All of these ways of stating the situation imply that we are likely to be tempted and need help. It seems to me that the two phrases belong together, and they might read: "Let us not be led into temptation, but deliver us from the tempter (or from the occasions that lead to temptation)."

The emphasis, therefore, is on "rescue us, save us from the forces of evil." There is recognition here both of the presence of temptation and of the tempting situations which we face. But there is also the identification of the tempter with the actual evil in the world. We see these powers of evil in the world, crushing our lives, spreading disease, encouraging hate, oppressing the powerless, and giving stones for bread. When we look into the slums of any city, the poverty of any rural area, the devasted lands of war-torn countries, the prisons and mental hospitals, and see the ruined lives of those who are children of God, surely we can pray for deliverance from evil. The words of the psalmist are reassuring:

> The Lord will guard you from all evil. . . .
> The Lord will guard your goings and comings henceforth
>     and for evermore" (Psm. 121:7-8,G).

These words also have in them the challenge and ring of a battle cry. They bring to mind the battle that is going on between God and the forces of evil. We need to rise up on the wings of God's power, we who are God's children, and join the battle against evil until it dies!

This is the simple body of the prayer. We pray that God's rule may be established on earth, that all people may have sufficient bread for the day, that we may be forgiven as we are forgiving, and that we may be spared from the forces of evil. In all these things, we confess our dependence upon God.

Then we rise up on the other wing of praise: "For thine is the kingdom, the power, and the glory, for ever and ever." It is believed by many that this is a later addition, but it balances this great model prayer and is true to its spirit. It brings us back to the adoration of the one true God in whom all things are possible—forever. Again, there is an echo of the voice of the psalmist:

"Lord, thou hast been our dwelling place
    in all generations . . .
    from everlasting to everlasting thou art God" (Psm. 90:1a,2b,RSV).

It is God in whom we live and move and have our being. We follow afar off when we seek to know or do God's will. Our souls are discordant and we seek to attune them in some kind of harmony with the Master Soul. All that we ask is a chance, a beggar's chance, to align our aims with God's aims, to live in commitment to those aims which we but dimly discern; and we have the right to ask that chance for all humankind.

> Lord of all being, throned afar,
> Thy glory flames from sun and star;
> Center and soul of every sphere,
> Yet to each loving heart how near![11]

The wings of prayer can lift us all to the level of God's presence, but when you pray, do not pray as the heathen do, for they believe that they will be heard if they use words enough. Be still, and let God come to you in the silence. Let your prayer affirm God's aims for you. Then let your loving adoration pour out in awe and wonder at the mystery of God's everlasting presence.

11. *Atlantic Monthly*, IV, December 1859, p. 766.

# 10
# *Where Is the Kingdom?*

The central teaching of Jesus was undoubtedly the kingdom of God. It stands at the beginning of his message where he said that we must repent because the kingdom is near at hand, and it remains the clue to his teaching throughout the synoptic record. The difficulty with the concept is that it has a number of different meanings, and it is hard to know what Jesus meant and what it should mean for us today.

In American Christianity, the meaning of the kingdom of God has changed from century to century. In the seventeenth century, the emphasis was almost entirely on the sovereignty of God, on God's absolute rule in the present situation. There was little thought of Utopian societies or of what people could do to improve the world. God was the sovereign who was to be obeyed. In the next century, the emphasis was on God's grace, on the kingdom in human hearts. This led to the desire for liberty, and the Quakers in particular stood for this interpretation. Here was the invisible kingdom pervading society with intangibles. There was emphasis on the conversion of the individual, and Christian freedom would lead to the community of love. Finally, there came the emphasis on the coming kingdom, with the accompanying hell-fire sermons, predictions of the end of the world, hope of filling the gap between human capacities and God's demands. This latter approach had a spin-off in the social Gospel, for only then could social crises be met.[1]

1. See H. Richard Niebuhr, *The Kingdom of God in America* (Chicago: Willett, Clark, 1937), pp. 51, 125, 135–136, 162.

H. Richard Niebuhr described this development of ideas concerning the kingdom as a symphony. No one pattern stood out, and there were gaps in the process. On the whole, however, each movement built on the previous one. "The first symphonic movement developed the theme of the sovereignty of God in many variations. There were discords and clashing of cymbals and some solo flights by wayward players in the orchestra, yet all were carried and united by the persistent strains of the first violins. The second movement began with the theme of Christ's kingdom for which the first part had prepared the listener. Sometimes only a fragment of the theme was sounded; a counter-theme of human kingdoms was developed; the movement was interrupted by rumbling kettledrums suggestive of internal strife. Yet the unity of the composition was maintained as crude instruments, fashioned in the backwoods and played by amateurs, reasserted the theme of the dominion of the Lord. The third movement was allegro. Though it began with forewarnings of doom a strain of hope lifted itself out of the morbid sounds and grew in power and completeness until it dominated the great polyphony of New World life."[2]

## THE KINGDOM OF GOD IN THE GOSPELS

Jesus believed that the kingdom of God was going to come in the near future. It would be a supernatural and catastrophic event which would transfigure and transform the present world. It would be a day of judgment, when those who were ready would be received into an earthly kingdom and those who had not repented would be cast into outer darkness. It is impossible to eliminate this element from Jesus' teachings, although the particular form in which it now appears reflects the hope of those early Christians whose preaching formed the basic structure and provided the content of the Gospels. Jesus expected God to act, and the results would be evident in this world. His was a *religious* hope of redemption for individuals and society. The message came directly from

2. Ibid., pp. 164–165.

his prophetic heritage rather than from the apocalyptic imagery of the Book of Enoch, although both traditions were probably involved.[3]

It is difficult to obtain a single idea of the kingdom from the Gospels, because a number of views had become popular by the time the Gospels were written. There were hopes for the future either in heaven or on earth; there were beliefs in the present realization of an inner kingdom; and there was identification of the kingdom with the church. The possibilities for Jesus can be reduced to two: (1) Jesus expected God to institute the new era on earth in the imminent future; or (2) he assumed that the world would go on and the kingdom would come through ethical redemption. It is difficult to harmonize these two views, and yet they stand side by side.

Amos N. Wilder calls attention to Rudolf Otto's observation that "men like Zoroaster, Mohammed, Jesus, see the kingdom arriving, but they act as if history were still going on."[4] The kingdom is present even when it is future. Jesus' teachings take account of both aspects of experience. Humanity stands under the judgment of God, yet humanity is not far from the kingdom when God's purposes are achieved; the kingdom is not here in its entirety and points to the future. There is a sense in which people have the kingdom in their midst, and at the same time the kingdom has not fully come. Persons by repentance prepare for the kingdom and by repentance they hasten the kingdom. The kingdom is God's, but humanity can take steps to bring it into existence. This is the religious basis for Christian ethics.[5] The eschatological framework led to an ethics of the kingdom, with absolutes not corrupted by necessary compromises of daily living in a nonideal situation.

Whenever God's love is operating with persuasive power, God is exercising sovereignty. No longer do we think of God as one who

3. See Frederick C. Grant, *Gospel of the Kingdom* (New York: Macmillan, 1940), pp. 14, 126, 131.

4. Amos N. Wilder, *Eschatology and Ethics in the Teaching of Jesus* (New York: Harper & Row, 1939), p. 35.

5. See ibid., pp. 73–77.

created the world from the outside and will one day step in to transform it. Just as God did not create the world in six days, so God will not change it in one. Our idea of time is nothing in the sight of God, although God works in and through the temporal order. But the purpose of Jesus' eschatology is still evident; it gives us a picture of God's reign as it affects human life. To say that we believe in the sovereignty of God, the ethical requirements of the kingdom, and the striving for social justice is not to stray from the fundamental principles of the kingdom which Jesus expressed within the first-century world view.

## THE SOVEREIGNTY OF GOD

God, says Whitehead, "is the poet of the world, with tender patience leading it by [the] vision of truth, beauty, and goodness."[6] God's tender care is such that nothing is lost, although God's judgment makes use of what is otherwise likely to be discarded. What is taken up into God is transformed and passed back into the world, and as this action is completed "the kingdom of heaven is with us today."[7] "The kingdom of heaven is not the isolation of good from evil. It is the overcoming of evil by good."[8]

God's aims for the world are prehended by us. But we still have to consent to the alignment of our aims with God's aim or to reject them. The relationship between God and us requires not only our commitment but our cooperation. But we are limited by our finiteness as well as our blindness and our self-willed obstinacy, so that we normally are not clear as to what God's will is. Furthermore, our human limitations lead to our failure to get higher than our own ideals. Therefore, we fall short of the demands that are placed upon us.

Within the framework of the kingdom, however, we need to recognize the priority of God's grace. God acts on individuals; this

6. Alfred N. Whitehead, *Process and Reality* (New York: Macmillan, 1929), p. 526.

7. Ibid., p. 532.

8. *Religion in the Making* (New York: Macmillan, 1926), p. 155.

activity overcomes evil with good and includes healing, reconciliation, and forgiveness; we are led into a fellowship which is a life of joy, symbolized by a banquet; and sinners are included in the fellowship. We may conclude, therefore, that "the experience of the kingdom is based on God's grace"[9] and leads to newness of life.

In the Lord's Prayer we pray, "Thine is the kingdom, the power, and the glory." This stresses the primacy of God. We may plant the seeds, meet the conditions, do the spadework, but God provides the growth. God brings about the increase of value through the emergence of novelty. God is present in the cosmos and in history and in our lives as sovereign. This does not mean that God's aims are not thwarted, or that the present stage of history meets with God's approval. We may be sure that it does not. God does not sanction evil and suffers from the results of human disobedience.

The *symbol* of eschatology stands for a present reality. God is related to historical processes, and sinful actions by human beings lead to judgment. God does not control historical actions directly by intervention, but the orderliness of the universe is God's way of control. God brings values into actuality through the works of those who are aligned with God's aims. God also seems to create new values through other than human channels, in spite of human opposition. Values are destroyed, however, when people go against the structures God has instituted in the world; this is the working of God's judgment.

If God is good and sovereign, those who desire the increase of good in the world must necessarily commit their programs and activities to the processes of God. As we look to the future, we can anticipate what each succeeding moment can mean, and this supports our motivation as we work toward the fulfillment of our goals. We can see the emergence of novelty and radical change, which threatens us even when it excites and satisfies us. Ultimately, life on this planet will become extinct, but in the meantime progress is both possible and desirable because it makes a difference to God

9. David R. Griffin, *A Process Christology* (Philadelphia: Westminstei Press, 1973), p. 201.

as well as to us. However, progress is not inevitable, although change is. The kingdom keeps coming when we find ourselves doing the work God has set up for us to do.

God's work can be done in a limited way by individuals, but to be effective in terms of peoples and nations there is needed a kind of cooperation that can come from the devotion of large numbers who share in the worship of God. There is much spadework to be done, and we still have to learn the conditions of social growth. But the time is at hand, and if we would save the present so-called Christian civilization by transforming it, there is an urgency just as great as that felt by the early Christians who expected the second coming of Christ.

## THE KINGDOM OF GOD AND ETHICS

The parables of the leaven and the mustard seed do not mean that the kingdom of God will come by a slow growth. These parables mean that the kingdom is as inevitable in its coming as the leaven is in affecting the whole loaf. God is able to work through the hearts of individuals to affect the whole of society, and to this extent the kingdom is already present. God's rule, sovereignty, or kingdom is evident wherever God's will is done.

This makes it clear that the concept of the kingdom is essentially ethical. *A complete turning about morally* is the meaning of repentance. One should repent because the kingdom of God is near. The parables often turn on God's seeking the lost and the lost turning about morally and returning to God. The revivalist's call of "Come to Jesus" or the cry of "Let Jesus come into your heart" are ways of expressing this fundamental truth. The whole idea of conversion, whether it be a violent change or a mild growth culminating in a decision, or whether it be a disclosure or a sense of the rule of Christ or the indwelling of the Holy Spirit, has been based on the belief that God's aims are moral and that these aims can take over or influence human aims. To this extent the rule or kingdom of God is realized.

159

The kingdom is *never fully realized in history*. The earlier forms of thinking about the end of the age or the breaking in of God at the conclusion of history is a way of making this clear. There is tension between God's ideal and eternal aims and what human beings can accomplish. One reason for human failure is that of finitude, so that we face what Reinhold Niebuhr called an "impossible possibility." There is also the unwillingness to make such an absolute commitment to the demands of love, with the risk that goes with such commitment. But chiefly, the tensions and challenges of life are so involved in relativities and the social situations are so mixed with evil that often the choice is between two evils. This is obviously apparent in the case of war, where the people have to choose between partaking in organized murder or being conscientious objectors whose refusal to fight results in injustice. Neither choice is right, but there is no satisfactory middle ground. Many options in the fields of economics and politics are such that the only possibilities open are seen ethically as shades of gray. It takes a certain kind of hardheadedness to deal with the art of the possible and still keep one's ethical sensitivity. There is a tension between the ideal and the possible, and the tension can only be relieved by conceiving of the highest ethical course of action as an approximation of God's will for us. But this is dangerous unless it is faced by the ideal, for we can reduce our actions to what is prudent and fail to have insight to see beyond our immediate interests. Thus, sin always pervades the actions of individuals in relation to society, and because of the interrelations of people with each other in all forms of social action, there is an important sense in which we may speak of corporate guilt. Christianity has always been identified with the poor, the outcast, and the oppressed, because we can see that there is a corporate responsibility for such people. There is no escape from the dilemma of moral individuals in an immoral society.

Yet Christianity changes people and therefore their relationship to society! The worldly do not know what it means to be "born again," and they would respond with the sarcasm of Nicodemus:

"How can a man be born again when he is old? Can he enter his mother's womb over again and be born?" (John 3:4,G). Nicodemus did not understand and took literally what was figurative language. But only those who refuse to look at the evidence can fail to see the work of God in the conversion of Paul, in the change that came over Augustine, in the work of Francis of Assisi. These are classic examples, worn thin by constant repetition; but there are people who come from the penitentiary, resolved that never again will they be tempted to violate laws against persons or property; there are those who have been drunk who turn from the alcoholic journey to paths of worthwhile living; there are those who have taken financial shortcuts in offices, banks, and politics, who confess what they have done and take the consequences, and then come back as responsible citizens. There are those who go through less dramatic changes as they discern various kinds and levels of wrongdoing and experience forgiveness, and then express their thanksgiving in a higher level of living.

This business of the kingdom or rule of God working in individuals is no small thing. It influences more than the individual who is most concerned. It permeates the whole realm of one's acquaintances and may lead others to change their lives. Attitudes are contagious, and the primary element in Jesus' teaching concerning salvation is having the right attitude. "Have the same attitude that Jesus Christ had," said Paul (Phil. 2:5,G). Wrong attitudes can lead to mass emotions, lynching parties, racial riots, and many other evils; and we can be swayed by mass propaganda on many such issues. Such an attitude takes courage: "Whatever happens," said Paul, "show yourselves citizens worthy of the good news of Christ" (Phil. 1:27,G). When we are fully committed to God and to what we consider to be God's aims, we will not be easily swayed by false gods, false prophets, and false attitudes.

Jesus' emphasis in his ethics was on the inner attitude, the intention. We know people by their actions, but only as a tree is inwardly healthy will it give forth good fruit. Furthermore, one is not judged so much by the quantity of the fruit as by the quality, and this is strictly a matter of inner health. That is why Jesus could speak of the widow's small gift as more important than the rich person's large gift. "The wind speaks not more sweetly to the giant oaks than to the least of all the blades of grass."[10] The source of such quality of life is God's grace, whether it is so recognized or not. We love because God first loved us. This is the specifically religious message of Jesus, and it inheres in all Christianity worthy of the name.

## THE KINGDOM AND SOCIETY

The idea of the kingdom is both personal and social. The rule of God is not just over individuals but also over society. God's will is to be done on earth, as it is in heaven. The hope is that God's rule will become universal. Again we come back to the insistence that absolute commitment to God, to the value structure and the process by which values emerge in the universe, is the only means by which the kingdom will come. It is a Utopian hope, kept alive because we see evidence of its partial realization from time to time.

There has always been divided opinion about the social implications of Christianity. Jesus had nothing to say specifically about social institutions, social interrelations, or social motives, although he was crucified with the charge of being "king of the Jews" in a society in which revolution was a constant possibility. His stress was upon human responsibility and not human rights. "Jesus dealt with no great problems such as war, slavery, morals, or government. His concern was with the immediate actions and reactions of individuals. He was concerned not with grandiose schemes but with given situations: with what people do or fail to do under actual pressure, if left alone, with the principles that motivate them, the reasons that restrain them. He treated people as though they were thoroughly competent. He told a parable here, enunciated a principle there, indicated a trend, a value, a consequence—and

10. Kahlil Gibran, *The Prophet* (New York: Knopf, 1923), p. 33.

went his way. He settled nothing, but in him we discover all life anew. He called it 'The Way.' Could it be possible that our crumbling world might find a new creative germ in this almost completely ignored and forgotten way?"[11]

This understanding of the Gospel does not destroy its social implications, but it clears up the misrepresentations of some promoters of the social Gospel, who have insisted that modern social techniques and political theories can be directly derived from biblical teachings. What we find are the principles of human relationships which are to be considered in the evaluations of any social, economic or political system, not the groundwork for socialism or guidelines for economic or political theories of this century.

The will of God is not any particular set of laws; it transcends every list of rules, including the Ten Commandments. The will of God is dynamic, not static. In the nature of God, there are unlimited potentialities for good, and, as these potentialities come upon the scene of human endeavor, the person who is committed to God will perceive these potentialities and will seek to realize them. This is the way that we come to know God's will for ourselves and act upon it.

Christians are not isolated individuals. They live in a society and belong to some branch of the church. As members of a Christian body they undertake responsibilities for those inside and outside the body. Yet the effectiveness of Christianity is hindered by what John C. Bennett has called *three half-truths:* (1) "Individuals can rise above any combination of social circumstances." (2) "Since individuals control institutions and social systems, it is enough to change individuals." (3) "You can change society without changing individuals." These three half-truths bring out the fundamental truth that "social change is both the condition and the fruit of individual salvation."[12]

---

11. Ray O. Miller, *The Pacific Churchman* (May 1940), p. 3.
12. John C. Bennett, *Social Salvation* (New York: Charles Scribner's Sons, 1935), pp. 44, 62.

If God works through persuasive love, and if we are charged with responsibility for the establishment of a just society, we need to understand the relation of power to love. Although power tends to corrupt, it is not necessarily evil and is a necessary factor in our understanding of conflict and order. God works in the world in relation to opposition and conflict. This opposition, like opposition between human beings, responds to power and coercion even when it does not respond to persuasion or love. But power and coercion are effective in a positive way when they are controlled by some understanding of law. There is need, therefore, for impersonal structures that determine to some degree the processes of an organism or society. As Whitehead put it, "Though life in its essence is the gain of intensity through freedom, yet it can also submit to canalization and so gain the massiveness of order."[13] There is a relationship between politics and sports, in that both are played according to agreed rules; there is conflict and each team faces opposition, but the right to compete is always recognized. Daniel Day Williams follows this illustration with the statement that "democracy as an ideal might be said to be the attempt to accord to every person the possibility of finding [one's] rightful share in the social good through an order in which [one's] interests and claims will have a fair hearing, and through a political process in which whatever power [one] can legitimately muster will be able to make itself felt."[14] This ideal points toward the emerging of values in the social order, but a realistic estimate of political activity leads to the conclusion that any use of power by an individual is useless until it is combined with the common cause of many others.

When the kingdom of God is restated in modern terms and applied to the society in which we live, the apocalyptic elements must be reinterpreted. The divine and catastrophic intervention predicted by the early church has not come to pass, and our contemporary knowledge of the processes of nature and of the working of God indicates that God's judgment works in a different way

13. *Process and Reality*, p. 164.
14. *God's Grace and Man's Hope* (New York: Harper & Row, 1949), p. 90.

from that presupposed in the New Testament. But the elements of threat, demand, and promise remain, for God's judgment works through natural channels according to the same standards. The change is that human responsibility is increased, for human beings who oppose God's will can frustrate God's rule. We are allowed to work out our own social salvation or damnation, and that is why the future seems so bleak.

The coming of the kingdom turns on the human sense of vocation, which has been defined as this: "The living God whose nature and purpose is love calls us to respond in our freedom to the tasks which are set for us by the fact that [God] is at work in our human history both as Creator and as Redeemer."[15] Many times the human following of this vocation will be focused on the mitigation of evil rather than the seeking of positive good, but always within the framework of the prayer: "Thy kingdom come."

## THE FUTURE

The future is open. There are no guarantees that there will be a last day when God takes over. If chance and novelty are operating principles of the universe and if human freedom is a crucial factor in the achievement of God's subjective aims, the future is not even known to God. When we anticipate our future, we are anticipating God's future as well. History is taken up into God's nature and transformed and becomes the basis for the future, so that the future never becomes static. Both God and the world "are in the grip of the ultimate metaphysical ground, the creative advance into novelty. Either of them, God and the World, is the instrument of novelty for the other."[16]

Yet there is a continuing connection between process and progress. Thus the goal is not static completion but continuing community, in which there is a real threat of judgment but also a pro-

15. Ibid., p. 147.
16. Whitehead, *Process and Reality*, p. 529.

mise of creative living. "Love does not ask for guarantees."[17] It of-fers a vision of deeper realities and greater belonging. It offers a hope of liberation from the rigid structures which imprison human hopes, which oppress human endeavors, and which promise a future hell rather than a heaven.

> Thy Kingdom, Lord, we long for,
> Where love shall find its own;
> And brotherhood triumphant
> Our years of pride disown,
> Thy captive people languish
> In mill and mart and mine;
> We lift to thee their anguish,
> We wait thy promised sign.[18]

We need to use all our insight, all our sensitive responses to unique situations, all our reason, and all our devotion in order to be open to God's working in the world. "Beloved, we are God's children now; it does not yet appear what we shall be" (I Jn 3:2,RSV). It is a slow process, and it will never be completely realized, for God is everlasting and what perishes will become the basis for a new becoming.

17. Daniel Day Williams, in Ewert H. Cousins, ed., *Hope and the Future of Man* (Philadelphia: Fortress, 1972), p. 88.

18. Vida Scudder (1905), in Caroline Hill, ed., *World's Great Religious Poetry* (New York: Macmillan, 1923), pp. 561–562.

# 11
# *What We Believe and What We Do*

Christianity has been both a set of beliefs and a way of life, and the two are permanently interwoven. Christianity is directly derived from Jesus of Nazareth. As his Jewish yet universal teachings came into contact with the Gentile world, beliefs about his person and his message were transformed into the thought patterns of Greek philosophy and Roman practicality. As the religion which bears his name spread throughout the world, a great variety of beliefs arose. Many of these beliefs were inconsistent with the original teachings and they contradicted each other, leading to various types of heresy and to divisions between churches in such areas as Egypt, Greece, Rome, and Syria. Some beliefs were crystallized by the formation of the canon of Scripture, councils, and groups seeking to preserve the primitive elements of the original Gospel. In all of these events there was development of belief, for Christianity is an *evolving religion*. It has been reinterpreted in succeeding ages to meet the needs and match the thought-forms and ideals of those periods.

It has been our purpose in the foregoing pages to indicate the *direction of belief and action that modern Christians should take.* These are not the only answers, but if the paradigm of process thought is combined with the use of empirical method and a careful evaluation of the Scriptures, the results should be much as outlined here. If the foundations for religious thinking are established, the superstructures can be constructed with some degree of confidence that they will not have to be torn down in the near future: they will need occasional alterations and modernizations as new developments occur.

The first developments of empirical method and process thought occurred early in this century, and then during the days of World War II and after there was an emphasis on the otherness of God and the centrality of revelation. But new developments indicate that we are ready for rethinking our beliefs on the basis of a different paradigm. Vatican II opened the door to theological rethinking among Roman Catholics, and the interest in Teilhard de Chardin stimulated thought along lines parallel to process thought. Today, some Catholic thinkers are using Whitehead's categories. Among Protestants there have been similar developments, although the history of such thinking goes back at least to Bergson and James.[1]

Important as believing is to Christians, we have never been satisfied with the emphasis on belief as a saving action. Christianity has always emphasized God's action and the human response in terms of grace and faith which issues in action. We speak of being saved by grace through faith, and therefore of being worthy of our vocation. Parallel to creedal affirmation has been the emphasis on the way of life. The primitive baptismal formula, "I believe that Jesus is the Christ," has always been balanced by the saying, "Behold how these Christians love one another."

## What We Believe

Christianity stands for the centrality of Christ. No theory of the incarnation is adequate, and many formulations have distorted Jesus' humanity. The fundamental element in Christology is that Jesus was the fullest possible revelation and manifestation of God in human nature. Jesus is important for what he tells us about God, so that we can agree with the words of the Fourth Gospel, "He who has seen me has seen the Father" (Jn 14:9,RSV). Through Jesus' life

1. See Randolph C. Miller, *The American Spirit in Theology* (Philadelphia: Pilgrim Press, 1974).

and work, God became more immanent in the world, and the presence of the Holy Spirit became more obvious.

Jesus is important for what he tells us about God. In a qualified way, we can speak of a Christ-model for God, for it preserves the interpersonal character of our relationship with God, our interdependence with nature, and our understanding of suffering love as central to God's character. The interpretation of Christ's atoning work points to the lost-found, alienation-rejection, death-resurrection motifs of religious living. Thus, God is seen as redeemer and reconciler, as giver of new life. Furthermore, because Jesus appears in history as the Christ, we come to an understanding of the interpretation of God as Lord of history as well as of nature and the cosmos. Finally, because of the contagious spirit engendered in Jesus, we are caught up in the lure of feeling which attracts us to God through him. In this sense, we are drawn psychologically to Jesus and through him to God.

God is spirit. The doctrine of the Holy Spirit has often been ignored or stated in inept terms, but from an empirical point of view the Holy Spirit is central. God in the consequent nature is immanent and is experienced. The primordial or abstract nature of God is not experienced except in the process of becoming concrete, as God's ingression into our lives. Thus, as we prehend God we are finding God in us as spirit. God dwells in and through the cosmos and therefore in human beings and is the ever-present sustainer of human beings in their striving after values. Vital Christianity has always stressed the presence of God *as spirit* in human endeavors, although the vocabularies may stress such models as "faith in Christ," "Christ in me," or "the attitude that Jesus Christ had." The words do not matter much, provided that the spirit which was in Jesus is in us.

With this doctrine about God as background, it is possible to develop an adequate understanding of the events of Christian living. Doctrines of sin, redemption, conversion, justification, and salvation need to be redefined in each age in order to have vital content. There is a sense of urgency in the Gospels which indicate that we must turn Godward before we perish, and in times of crisis this aspect stands out compellingly. The doctrine of the kingdom of God stands before us as an invitation, a challenge, a promise, and a judgment.

Human beings are commanded to love both God and other human beings, and the commands are *equal*. This tells us a good deal about the worth of every person and about the expectations for noble living. No matter what one's doctrine of sin may be, there is the conviction of the actual and potential worth of every human being. Salvation is a possibility for everyone. Human beings belong to a complex of relationships that includes God. We are capable of free choice in both thinking and acting, and yet we are limited by what we have been and what we are becoming. We live by the consequences of our own actions and the actions of others. Ultimately, our lives include risk and adventure, and our value to God is that we are capable of aligning ourselves with God's initial aim for all human beings.

We need to belong; we need other people as well as God for our fulfillment; we need to express our sense of worth through ministry to other human beings; we need to worship together, for this is our primary response to the everlasting presence of God. So we need a church. We come together sharing enough common beliefs and convictions to make us a community, and we are brought closer together by the power that God exerts in and through our worship. This leads to personal, moral, social, and political action as our way of aligning our aims with God's persuasive love.

In this coming together, we affirm our common allegiance. This is what the historic creeds have done in the past. In the midst of confused thought and threatened heresies, the creeds aided in systematizing beliefs and in excluding those who altered the essential Christian doctrines. Today the creeds stand as inherited statements, as symbols of loyalty, and although the beliefs are expressed in terms of outmoded science and philosophy, the fundamental story that is told is sound. When the creeds are seen as symbols of a common commitment rather than as a guide for specific beliefs, they serve a liturgical purpose that is effective today.

But creeds are often understood as tests of belief, and as such the traditional creeds are obviously outmoded. Attempts have been made to create new creeds, but none has proved satisfactory to any large number of Christians. In an attempt to make a generalized and biblical statement, the English modernists presented a creed based on the Johannine writings that commended itself to a number of people. This version is slightly altered:

We believe in God:
God is Spirit, and we worship God in spirit and in truth.
God is Light, and if we walk in the light as God is in the light, we
     have fellowship with one another.
God is Love, and we who love God are born of God and know
     God.
Jesus is the Son of God, and God has given us eternal life, and this
     life is in the Son.
We are the children of God, and God has given us the Spirit.
If we confess our sins, God is faithful and just to forgive us our sins.
The world passes away and the lust of it, but we who do the will of
     God abide forever.[2]

This creed stresses the relationships between human beings and God, but does not spell out theological details or ethical demands. We cannot be too straitlaced about the content of theology, providing it does not do violence to the fundamentals. The traditional creeds are *valid insofar as they can be proved by Scripture*, but today there is some confusion about the essential teachings of Scripture, although through the developments of biblical scholarship we are gaining more accurate information. The newer creeds need not replace the old ones, providing that we see the older ones as symbols of loyalty rather than as tests of orthodoxy.

2. Original in H. D. A. Major, *Church's Creeds and the Modern Man* (London: Skeffington, 1933), p. 108.

A theology for today must be free of inert ideas that fail to produce meaning for what we experience. It must be both relevant and communicable, and therefore it must provide guidance for both belief and action. We must remember that *justification does not come by belief, but by faith, which is the absolute commitment of the total self to the reality of God.*

## What We Do

Primitive Christianity was known as "The Way." The earliest followers of Jesus Christ were not known so much for their professions of belief as for the way they behaved. The courage of these men and women in the face of persecution, the steadfastness of their activities, their devotion to each other, and their loyalty to God earned them the respect of the non-Christians. They were willing to take strong stands on ethical issues, on the kinds of jobs that met their standards, on political loyalty and even loyalty oaths. They were considered to be subversive by the authorities, for they claimed that their primary loyalty was to Christ rather than to the emperor. They expected to get into trouble, to be thrown into jail, and to be put to death, and in many cases their expectations were fulfilled.

There is an ethical quality in Christian living; there is a moral rigor in the expectation that we should love both God and our neighbors as ourselves. This style of life based on the implications of love makes Christianity distinctive and operative. Because God loves us, we are to express that same love in our daily lives. It is easy to reduce those requirements to specific duties, such as the disciplinary requirements for receiving communion, belonging to a specific denomination with its undemanding expectations, or even doing acts of penance. These things may be important as spiritual exercises, but they are never ends in themselves. The works which followers of "The Way" are expected to do are those which aid in hastening the time when God's rule will be more fully established. This involves a revolutionary social Gospel as well as radical change in individuals. *A valid Christianity seeks to permeate and influence its whole human environment!*

The Christian seeks to be aligned with God's aims for the world. As we adjust ourselves to those processes which increase value in the world, our own goals are changed and our own lives are enriched. Those processes are at work, whether we recognize them or not, and by our alignment with them new channels are opened up through which God works more effectively than before. Each of us has the potentiality to become God's agent. As more of us are committed to God's will, the kingdom comes nearer to realization. Our salvation and the salvation of the world depend upon the relationship with God that leads to a greater degree of love and righteousness.

All of this is very general, for in the last analysis each of us has to decide how God's aims and ours are to be aligned in each decision. Just as no one can do our believing for us, so no one can make a commitment for us or act for us. This is the freedom of the individual person which God never takes from us. We can give up that freedom, but even that is our free act. As God's aims become specific in each situation, we have to work it out. There are general principles to help us, some of which have been enunciated above, but beyond that we are on our own—with God.

Christianity has been at its best in times of crisis. Like all religions, Christianity has been damned by its fair-weather friends. It has let itself be identified too closely with the state and political systems, with economic privilege, with traditional moral standards, and with Western imperialism. It has been caught up in racism, sexism, and nationalism. But Christianity took hold in a dying Greek culture, it preserved the best of Roman culture after the decline of the empire, it served as a basis for cohesion in the difficult times during the exploration and settling of the United States, and it holds a message for the Western world today as that world goes into a moral and political decline. The combination of optimism and pessimism, of striving and peace, of abundance and tragedy, which are synthesized in the Christian hope, is the result of almost two thousand years of human history and experience. The sufferings of this present time are probably no worse than past sufferings, and the hope of what is in store for humanity exceeds all visions of streets of gold. We are children of God now, "and it does not yet appear what we shall be."

When one is fully committed to the will of God as revealed in Jesus Christ, and is ready to learn more fully what God's will is, that person is a Christian. Quite naturally the Christian will seek for fellowship with others in *a* church, and so will become a member of *the* church. By God's grace, such a person will become more fully attuned to those processes which make for value in the world, helped by prayer and corporate worship, as well as by the fellowship which includes the individual in the group. Thus, one comes into the promise of the abundant life, based on values that are different from the usual expectations of a materialistic society.

## OUR CULTURAL HERITAGE AND RESPONSIBILITY

Christianity is our cultural heritage. It speaks to us not only from a point 1900 years ago, for the entire 1900 years of its history carry a message which we dare not ignore today. It relates to our individual situations, of course, but it also permeates the society in which we live. The nucleus of Western civilization is Christian, however much that culture seems to have strayed from it, and this is particularly so in the case of American democracy. It is because of the paramount importance of Christianity for the future of ourselves and our culture that the problem of the beliefs that we can hold today is essential to us both as Christians and as individuals.

*Christianity is true.* Throughout the history of our religion there has always been *a central tradition,* avoiding excesses on the one side and then on the other, which has proved defensible according to the standards of philosophy, values, and common sense. It has

174

been based solidly on Scripture and tradition, and yet has been open to the new discoveries of human experiment and reason. Attacks on Christianity have led to the assertion of extreme positions; social conditions have brought about emphases on those aspects of Christianity which were most helpful in meeting those positions, which today have led quite properly to emphases on the oppressed, blacks, and women as the focus of the application of theology; and the temper of the times has resulted in extremes of either rationalism or irrationalism. Modern Barthianism is a contemporary example of a one-sided message which was helpful under limited conditions. Barth's position was developed in the light of a rising totalitarianism, under social conditions which reflected disillusionment with Christian socialism and an ultraliberal theology, and as a reaction against an easy liberalism and faith in science. It was a projection of the fascist formula into the skies and at the same time a denial of that formula in politics. It was an irrational reaction that provided hope under the stress of pessimism about human possibilities in the face of oppression, and therefore placed the responsibility for escape on God. It is this last emphasis on the absolute sovereignty of a wholly other God that made Barth's message relevant to those who were otherwise helpless. It was as extreme in its way as the humanistic teaching that human beings could do anything they desired without reliance on God which led finally to an equally unrealistic pessimism.

Although these one-sided statements are helpful under certain conditions, the central Christian tradition, with its sanity and balance, provides a sense of the enduring worth of Christianity. A Barthian emphasis is needed only when the central tradition has lost its flexibility and therefore fails to meet the needs of the people. Throughout these pages, we have been looking at an interpretation of the essential teaching of Christianity seen within an empirical and process framework, trying to keep the balance between undue pessimism and cynicism on the one hand and an unfounded optimism and unrealistic expectations on the other. We have pointed to the difference between the human and divine contributions to the establishment of God's reign and have tried to be realistic about our social and religious hopes. The central tradition of Christianity must never become crystallized, because the power of the Christian religion lies in its ability to meet human beings where they are and to lead them on to what they may become. Inert beliefs, no matter how hallowed with time, do not serve this program. But when faith, based on the right beliefs that are adequately established, provides that commitment which leads to action in the service of God, there is reason to hope that at least in God's sight things will turn out right in the end.

Belief in God and in many of the details of the Christian tradition can be established in the courts of experience and reason, at least in part, and *we trust the God we know in part.* When Jesus said that we must be as children in order to be saved, he was not thinking of childish beliefs, but of childlike trust in one's parents. If we trust God in the way that children trust their parents, we can be led by God into the kingdom.

*Christianity helps individuals.* There are resources in every human being which remain untouched. These hidden potentialities remain hidden because there is no stimulus to bring them into actuality. Sometimes devotion to a cause will bring them to light. The higher the cause the more likely that they will be uncovered. Christianity, because it points to God who is "the lure of feeling," attracts the best in us. There is a powerful affection that can delve into the unconscious and draw out of us those activities, thoughts, and relations which serve the increase of value in the world.

Of course, a lukewarm devotion even to a higher goal will not be effective against lower goals backed by greater zeal. Often, throughout history, Christianity has faced rivals with higher motivation: Moslems in some areas, Nazis in others, and Communists. Christians need the reinforcement of other Christians to keep their loyalty alive. A program to stimulate sensitivity to values, to see values in their completeness, to make them efficient as they are carried from the potential to the actual state, and to lead to a progression of values so that no achievement is seen as final should be part of the church's life.

Christianity is a religion of power, but that power is in terms of persuasion rather than force. It captures its devotees by its inherent appeal to the image of God in every person. When Christians rely on mass baptisms, on force rather than informed teaching, and on indoctrination rather than education, they are not being true to their convictions, for only through the freedom of consent does any person truly commit the self to God.

This reliance on persuasive love is both the strength and the weakness of Christianity. In social and political action, belief in love leads to a tension between what is and what ought to be, and the Christian faces the dilemma of refusing to take part in social action involving force (as the pacifist in case of war), or of granting that the support of one force against another is a compromise involving the admission of sin. Neither answer is satisfactory, but the power of God's love works through people in such situations providing they do not deify their solution to the dilemma. God's forgiveness helps those who know their decisions are compromises; but when people insist that theirs is the absolutely Christian answer, they deny the dilemma and refuse to recognize the tension in every decision. Here again we must judge ourselves by the degree of our sensitivity to the will of God in each unique situation.

When we have the strength and courage to overcome obstacles which face us, this power is a gift of God, even though it may also be the stimulation of latent energies, a glandular reaction, or the result of prayer. When we have the patience and comfort of accepting what is inevitable, without distortion of our visions or our honest hopes, that, too, is a gift of God. And the ability to determine which should be overcome and which should be accepted is a gift of wisdom, for this insight into possibilities as distinguished from dreams is a gift of God to every person who keeps sensitive, aware, and curious, using every power of discernment to exhaust the alternatives and then making a final decision with full trust in God. We may believe that "with God all things are possible" and "that all things work for good for them that love God," and at the same time realize that all things are not possible *for us* in the providence of God.

When we fulfill God's conditions, it is God's purpose which is affirmed, and these may be different from our desires. As God prehends us, our ideals and values are taken into the consequent nature where they are transformed. As God's ways and thoughts are different from ours, so are God's ways and thoughts higher than ours, and in placing ourselves in God's love and care we dedicate ourselves to the highest that we can conceive, and know that the mystery of God transcends and transforms our thoughts.

Christianity speaks to us where we are. Jesus had a custom, embarrassing to the leaders of his time, of seeking out people in the lower stations of life. But he did not mix with winebibbers just for the conviviality of the occasion, for he always reached them at that point and then drew them to himself. He had dinner with a dishonest tax collector, and as a result the man paid back to everyone more than he had taken from them. Jesus did not tell him what to do; he simply showed his love and let events take their course. In the case of the adulterous men, Jesus let them convict themselves of sin, and then he turned to the woman and did not condemn her. With men and women alike, Jesus was looking for the potential for faith, and when he found it the result was a healing and a restoring to their full humanity. This is what happens to any person who exposes one's self to the love of God.

When Christianity is true to itself, it does not impose restrictions and blue laws. It is, as Whitehead said, "a little oblivious to morals." Jesus never worried overmuch about the laws of the Sabbath or food. He said that we should not be anxious about food and drink, or clothes, but to compare the way God treats the sparrows and the lilies of the field with the way God treats people. With the elimination of anxiety, we are free to be open to God and to seek for those values which take us beyond the restrictions of legal restraints.

There is much to be said for moral integrity, for goodness and courage and honesty, and these are essential for a life of commitment to God, but I wonder if, when all is said and done, the clue to Christian living is not *radiance*. There is a style of life that has a contagion about it, that draws others to the one who has it. It is not an accident that Jesus is pictured with a halo around his head, and that angels, flashing stars, fine gems, and spices became part of the birth stories. The religious imagination was working to say something through such vivid imagery, and we respond to the radiance of the picture that is drawn. In Christian living there shines the radiance as of a gem, reflecting the glory of God as a gem reflects the sunlight. There is much darkness in life, but the radiance of Jesus shines through. It is this captivating radiance which makes us be born anew. We are drawn or lured to God by a feeling that is responding to a persuasion that is greater than our self-centered desires, and in our decision to trust God's way and accept God's aims, we partake of the abundant life. This abundance is expressed as blessedness or happiness. The New Testament has many references to joy. We may "leap for joy" or have the "joy and peace of believing." The promise is for a life full of radiance and joy.

*Christianity and society.* If the Christianity which is true and the Christ who is radiant are translated into the prosaic realm of the work of God in history, we have a problem. From the perspective of history, we can see that every culture has had a religious nucleus and that there was a correlation between the condition of this motivating center and that of the civilization itself. When this center loses its power, the civilization will crumble. This has happened many times in the history of the world.

We do not have the techniques and powers to bring a nation under God's rule, but the knowledge that a nation has a religious nucleus provides a starting point. It tells us that artificial creations are almost impossible to achieve except in anti-Christian and totalitarian states, for the genius of Christianity is to work through the free decisions of individuals and groups. When even a small number of people was nominally Christian, it was possible to establish in the new United States a democracy on a religious basis, even though it was a secularized version of classical Protestantism.

It is obvious that Christianity is a less potent force in the United States than it was a generation or two ago, and there is no reason to assume that Christianity is less likely to be discarded than it has been in Communist countries. The disarray in the churches, combined with a growing secular interpretation of events, is not a hopeful sign. However, a renewal of Christianity is not an impossibility; it has happened several times in the past 1900 years. The problem today is to overcome the weakness within Christianity and the challenge of secularism.

Even those religious groups that are growing do not provide much hope. Most of them take a pessimistic view of the nation; in some cases they have an apocalyptic outlook that avoids political responsibility, for the end of the world will come with the corruption of the nation. The Oriental and other non-Christian sects, as well as some Christian groups, ignore political realities. They have no faith in rational views and prefer to rely on immediate experience. There is no planning for the long run, no sense of democratic procedures, and no desire to reform the world.

There were some social radicals for a time who sought to change things. Many of them were alienated from churches and synagogues but had caught the idealism of Christian and Jewish teachings. Led by dynamic ministers, priests, and rabbis, these young people could not make a dent on the political machines, and their protests led to the killings of students at Jackson State and Kent State. Disillusioned and broken in spirit, they have become the quiet and disengaged who are in many cases adapting to the mores of current society.

The churches and synagogues have also been caught up in a civil religion that tends to bless the American way. The symbol of this was the services in the White House with guest (read "captive") preachers. A kind of Americanism developed that transcended denominational and faith barriers, and such a love of things American led to the loss of critical powers. There are many people in the main line churches and synagogues who reject social reform in favor of such civil religion, saying that politics and religion do not mix, or the business of the church is religion, or "stick to the Gospel."

Any prophecy of what will happen is futile. The future is open. Within American Christianity there are traditions of revival, renewal, and development. There are pressures for such renewal, especially from Latin American countries which see Christianity as needing association with a critical consciousness which assists the peasant in asserting full humanity. What Paulo Freire calls "conscientization" is taking hold in some parts of the world, especially in the field of Christian education. A sensitivity to the needs of those who are outcast from the mainstream of social living, which has always been part of Christianity, has been increasingly focused on blacks, Chicanos, and women in this country, and on the peasant population in many countries. The churches have learned to work together through the National Council of Churches and the World Council of Churches along these lines, and in time it may be that the power structures in local congregations will see that this is part of ministry. But it must be more than traditional "charity" or occasional fasts to help the hungry. The world situation, as well as that of the United States, is too precarious for patchwork solutions.

God's aims for the United States are not immediately obvious. The situation is complex. The problem of hunger is complexly related to those of population control and the possibility of work, so that economics and religion are intimately bound together. We tend to place our faith in technical breakthroughs, but the problem is not just one of engineering. Robert L. Heilbronner suggests that the chance of doomsday is present, unless a "post-industrial" society evolves. This "requires nothing less than the gradual abandonment of the lethal techniques, the uncongenial lifeways, and the dangerous mentally of industrial civilization itself."[3] In today's

3. Robert L. Heilbronner, *An Inquiry into the Human Prospect* (New York: W. W. Norton, 1974), p. 138.

society, "the creative advance into novelty" could be smothered by a static structure. Yet radical change is necessary for survival. Robert Bellah writes that "the inward reform of conversion, the renewal of an inward covenant among the remnant that remains faithful to the hope for rebirth, is more necessary than it has ever been in America. The great experiment may fail utterly, and such failure will have dark consequences not only for Americans but for all the world."[4]

If we can hear the call of God in this situation, if enough of us respond in terms of political and social responsibility, if we search for the greatest wisdom in the face of almost impossible problems, then there will be hope for the future of the earth. If disaster comes, then the hope will remain with the remnant of the faithful, who may become the energizing heart of some new civilization in the future. Although we must learn how to use political power and to work for political change, this is not enough unless we come to a new view of human nature. Unless we have a vision of what life, liberty, and the pursuit of happiness means for every human being, we will not solve our problems by attaining these goals for ourselves. We need a new reformation.

## CHRISTIANITY AND GOD

God is the center of all religions, for religion is the human attempt to relate to whatever has the power to sustain and transform human beings in their spiritual quest. In this sense, all religions have some degree of revelation in them. In Christianity, the primary revelation is found in Jesus Christ; and this makes a great difference, for by seeing God in the face of Jesus Christ we believe that God works through persuasive love to bring the children into the kingdom. It is the Christian concept of God as rooted in Jesus Christ as a model that marks Christianity off from 'other world

4. Robert N. Bellah, *The Broken Covenant* (New York: Seabury, 1975), pp. 162–163.

religions. We think about God in terms of Christ, but we worship the God *of* Jesus Christ. Our faith is in the faith of Jesus, and yet we develop a faith of our own.

The most important element in Christianity is God, for God is the source of our being and cannot be destroyed. As long as God is, there is a basis for hope. God is all that counts in the end, and if we know God and commit our total selves to God, all fear is cast out and we do not become anxious even though we perish. The musical *Godspell* ends with the prayer, "Long live God!"

Our importance is derived from God. There is little about us that makes us more significant than other animals except that we are children of God who have certain endowments which God has given us. At the lowest level of humanity there is not much difference between cannibalism and eating a lamb, except for the value that God has placed on us. It is a false humanism that assumes the ultimate value of human personality unless we realize that God is the one who makes the value judgment. This is why we can say that human beings are created in the image of God.

It is because of the value that God places on us that we may believe in immortality. If God has made us "a little lower than God," we do not believe that God would allow so valuable a being to perish. If God is good and a conserver of goods, and if we have value in the sight of God, then God will not let us be destroyed. This is the logic of belief in immortality. There is nothing about us that can determine whether we will become immortal. The evidence does not lie in us but in the nature of God as a valuer of persons. The Christian tradition has interpreted these beliefs in terms of personal or subjective immortality or life after death, but process thought leads to an objective immortality where the values and thoughts and deeds of our lives are prehended by God who is everlasting.

We may have fleeting glimpses of what we call immortality. In worship, we have experiences of being uplifted by a power we cannot see. We respond to great music by saying that we have looked into the heart of the Eternal. Ethical actions of sacrifice and mar-

183

tyrdom by others are perceived as having everlasting significance. We are caught up in complex situations and make decisions that have permanent effects on our lives and the lives of others. A mother sometimes feels this tremendous significance of the moment with the birth of a child. It is an achievement that may come in a time of crisis, as men and women rise to heights of heroism in the face of pestilence, floods, earthquakes, and wars. It comes to all of us as we keep faith with ourselves and with God in each passing situation. We align ourselves with God's aims as best we can, and God acts through grace to give us the creative, transforming, and healing power that makes for a radiant and abundant life. We are comrades of Jesus Christ, heirs of God and joint heirs with Christ, through whom we find the abundant life. All that we do and are continues to be meaningful in the memory of God.[5]

Human hopes are expressed in many ways. Historically, Christianity has provided hope for the suffering and the oppressed, but the churches have not always been sensitive to these needs. Today's racial problems are still difficult. The economic future is bleak for many workers, especially those in the Third World. The feminist movement is based on the belief that in Christ "there is neither male nor female." There are ecological and energy problems which threaten our existence. Yet there is an "earnest expectation," an "eager longing," for "the whole creation is on tiptoe" as we hope to see the children of God "coming into their own" (see Rom. 8:19).

Hope remains steadfast in the human heart because hope has been placed there by God. "God is our hope and strength. . . . Therefore we will not fear." We are the children of God, and nothing can separate us from the love of God. We are comrades of Jesus Christ, in whom is love and life. We are those who are living the abundant life now, and it does not yet appear what we shall be, for that is in the hand of God.

---

5. See Randolph C. Miller, *Live Until You Die* (Philadelphia: Pilgrim Press, 1973), pp. 111–131.

# Books to Read

The following books are recommended and were in print when going to press, except as noted. Their level of difficulty is indicated [(*) simple to read, (†) somewhat difficult, (††) technical].

## 1  YOUR FAITH AND MINE

*Barbour, Ian G. *Myths, Models and Paradigms.* New York: Harper & Row, 1974.

†Cousins, Ewert H., ed. *Process Theology.* New York: Newman, 1971.

*Hamilton, Peter N. *The Living God and the Modern World.* Philadelphia: Pilgrim Press, 1967.

*Mellert, Robert B. *What Is Process Theology?* New York: Paulist, 1975.

*Pittenger, W. Norman. *Trying to Be a Christian.* Philadelphia: Pilgrim, 1972.

†Schilling, Harold K. *The New Consciousness in Science and Religion.* Philadelphia: Pilgrim, 1973.

## 2  HOW TO TEST OUR BELIEFS

*Barbour, Ian G., ed. *Science and Religion.* New York: Harper & Row, 1968.

*James, William. *Varieties of Religious Experience.* New York: Longmans, Green, 1902. Many editions available.

†Miller, Randolph C. *The American Spirit in Theology.* Philadelphia: Pilgrim. 1974.

†Smith, John E. *Experience and God.* New York: Oxford, 1968.

†Smith, John E. *Religion and Empiricism.* Milwaukee: Marquette University Press, 1967.

### 3 & 4   WHAT GOD DOES and WHO IS GOD?

†Birch, Charles. *Nature and God.* Philadelphia: Westminster, 1966.

†Cobb, John B., Jr. *God and the World.* Philadelphia: Westminster, 1969.

*Holmes, Urban T., III. *To Speak of God.* New York: Seabury, 1974.

*Macquarrie, John. *Thinking about God.* New York: Harper & Row, 1975.

†Miller, Randolph C. *The Language Gap and God.* Philadelphia: Pilgrim, 1970.

†Whitehead, Alfred N. *Religion in the Making.* New York: Macmillan, 1926; Meridian 1960.

### 5   WHO WAS JESUS?

†Bornkamm, Günther. *Jesus of Nazareth.* New York: Harper & Row, 1960.

*Cadbury, Henry J. *The Peril of Modernizing Jesus.* New York: Macmillan, 1937; Allenson, 1962.

*Sloyan, Gerard S. *Jesus on Trial.* Philadelphia: Fortress, 1973.

*Smith, Charles W. F. *The Jesus of the Parables.* Philadelphia: Pilgrim, 1975.

*Wahlberg, Rachel Conrad. *Jesus According to a Woman.* New York: Paulist/Deus, 1975.

### 6   WHAT ABOUT CHRIST?

†Griffin, David R. *A Process Christology.* Philadelphia: Westminster, 1974.

†Knox, John. *Humanity and Divinity in Christ.* Cambridge: Cambridge University Press, 1967.

†McIntyre, John. *The Shape of Christology.* Philadelphia: Westminster, 1966.

†Niebuhr, H. Richard. *Christ and Culture*. New York: Harper & Row, 1951.

*Pittenger, W. Norman. *Christology Reconsidered*. London: SCM Press, 1970.

## 7  WHY BELIEVE IN THE CHURCH?

†Lee, Bernard. *The Becoming of the Church*. New York, Paulist 1974.

†Miller, Randolph C. *Christian Nurture and the Church*. New York: Scribners, 1961 (out of print).

††Minear, Paul S. *Images of the Church in the New Testament*. Philadelphia: Westminster, 1960.

*Pittenger, W. Norman. *The Christian Church as a Social Process*. Philadelphia: Westminster, 1971.

†Williams, Colin W. *New Directions in Theology Today Vol. 4: The Church*. Philadelphia: Westminister. 1968.

## 8  ON BEING HUMAN

*Averill, Lloyd J. *The Problem of Being Human*. Valley Forge: Judson, 1974.

*Menninger, Karl. *What Ever Became of Sin?* New York: Hawthorn, 1973.

*Miller, Randolph C. *Live Until You Die*. Philadelphia: Philadelphia, 1973.

†Pannenberg, Wolfhart. *What Is Man?* Philadelphia: Fortress, 1970.

†Russell, Letty M. *Human Liberation in a Feminist Perspective—A Theology*. Philadelphia: Westminster, 1974.

†Shinn, Roger L. *New Directions in Theology Vol. 5: Man, The New Humanism*. Philadelphia: Westminister, 1968

## 9  DOES PRAYER WORK?

*Bloy, Myron B. Jr., ed. *Search for the Sacred*. New York: Seabury, 1972.

*Cox, Harvey. *The Feast of Fools*. Cambridge: Harvard University Press, 1969; Harper & Row, 1971.

*Kirby, John C., ed. *Word and Action.* New York: Seabury, 1969.

*Nouwen, Henri. *Reaching Out.* New York: Doubleday, 1975.

*White, James F. *New Forms of Worship.* Nashville: Abingdon, 1971.

## 10   WHERE IS THE KINGDOM?

†Beardslee, William A. *A House for Hope.* Philadelphia: Westminster, 1972.

†Cousins, Ewert H., ed. *Hope and the Future of Man.* Philadelphia: Fortress, 1972.

†Hebert, A. Gabriel. *God's Kingdom and Ours.* London: SCM Press, 1959; Allenson, 1959.

†Niebuhr, H. Richard. *The Kingdom of God in America.* Chicago: Willett, Clark, 1937; Harper & Row, 1959.

†Williams, Daniel Day. *God's Grace and Man's Hope.* New York: Harper & Row, 1949, 1965.

## 11   WHAT WE BELIEVE AND WHAT WE DO

†Barbour, Ian G., ed. *Earth Might Be Fair.* Englewood Cliffs, New Jersey: Prentice-Hall, 1972.

*Bellah, Robert N. *The Broken Covenant.* New York: Seabury, 1975.

*Bennett, John C. *The Radical Imperative.* Philadelphia: Westminister, 1975.

†Bock, Paul. *In Search of a Responsible World Society.* Philadelphia: Westminster, 1974.

†Freire, Paulo. *Education for a Critical Consciousness.* New York: Seabury, 1973.

*Marty, Martin. *The Pro & Con Book of Religious America.* Waco: Word, 1975.

## MORE TECHNICAL BOOKS

††Baum, Gregory. *Man Becoming.* New York: Seabury, 1970.

††Brown, Delwin; James, Ralph E., Jr.; and Reeves, Gene. *Process Philosophy and Christian Thought.* Indianapolis: Bobbs-Merrill, 1971.

†Clebsch, William A. *American Religious Thought: A History.* Chicago: University of Chicago Press, 1973.

††Cobb, John B., Jr. *A Christian Natural Theology.* Philadelphia: Westminster, 1965.

†Dahl, Nils, A. *The Crucified Messiah.* Minneapolis: Augsburg, 1975.

††Hartshorne, Charles. *A Natural Theology for Our Time.* LaSalle, Illinois: Open Court, 1967.

††Hartshorne, Charles. *The Divine Relativity.* New Haven: Yale University Press, 1948, 1964.

††Kelsey, David H. *The Uses of Scripture in Recent Theology.* Philadelphia: Fortress, 1975.

††McClinton, James William, Jr., and Smith, James M. *Understanding Religious Convictions.* Notre Dame: University of Notre Dame Press, 1975.

†Meland, Bernard E., ed. *The Future of Empirical Theology.* Chicago: University of Chicago Press, 1969.

†Meland, Bernard E. *The Realities of Faith.* New York: Oxford University Press, 1962.

††Niebuhr, Reinhold. *The Nature and Destiny of Man.* 2 vol. New York: Scribners, 1941, 1942, 1949.

††Ramsey, Ian T. *Christian Empiricism.* Grand Rapids, Michigan: Eerdmans, 1974.

††Ramsey, Ian T., ed. *Words about God.* New York: Harper & Row, 1971.

††Ogden, Schubert M. *The Reality of God.* New York: Harper & Row, 1966.

†Overman, Richard. *Evolution and the Christian Doctrine of Creation.* Philadelphia: Westminster, 1967.

††Temple, William. *Nature, Man and God.* London: Macmillan, 1934.

††Whitehead, Alfred N. *Adventures of Ideas.* New York: Macmillan, 1933; Free Press.

††Whitehead, Alfred N. *Process and Reality.* New York: Macmillan, 1929; Free Press, 1949.

††Wieman, Henry N. *Religious Experience and Scientific Method.* New York: Macmillan, 1926; Southern Illinois University Press, 1972.

††Wieman, Henry N. *Seeking a Faith for a New Age.* Metuchen, New Jersey: Scarecrow, 1975.

††Wieman, Henry N. *The Source of Human Good.* Chicago: University of Chicago Press, 1946; Southern Illinois University Press, 1964.

†Williams, Daniel Day. *The Spirit and Forms of Love.* New York: Harper & Row, 1968.

# Index

Page references for more important treatment are in boldface type.

193